BILLY B. GOOD'S

Fun Facts
and
Triva Snacks

Volume 1

Copyright 2022 by Billy B. Good/Profound Impact Group, LLC

All rights reserved. No part of this book may be reproduced in any form or by any electronic or mechanical means, including information storage and retrieval systems, without permission in writing from the publisher, except in the case of brief quotations contained within critical articles and reviews.

Books may be purchased in quantity by contacting the publisher directly:

Profound Impact Group, LLC

P.O. Box 506

Alpharetta, GA 30009

Info@ProfoundGroup.com

ISBN:

978-1-942151-16-6 (Print)

978-1-942151-17-3 (ebook)

978-1-942151-18-0 (audio)

Cover design: Damonza

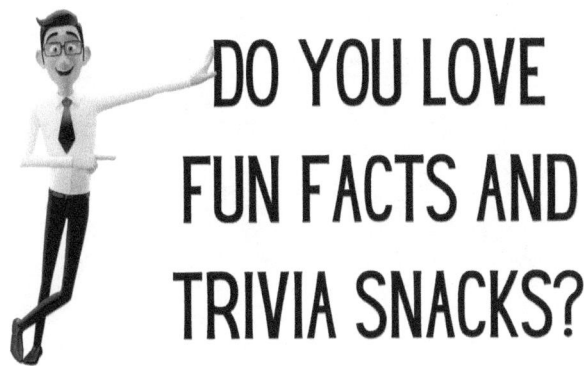

DO YOU LOVE FUN FACTS AND TRIVIA SNACKS?

Most email sucks. This does not.

Subscribe to Billy B. Good. It takes about 27 seconds.
Then you'll finally get the good stuff in your inbox.
And, you'll get a free ebook, too!

Sign up at
BillyBGood.com

 # But first...

I put the word 'trivia' in the title of this book and I don't even like that word. To me it implies a sense of "not important." Which, with some trivia, may be true.

But if you probe a smidge deeper, you'll find the good stuff, the stuff that makes the stark facts interesting.

That's why I don't care for trivia books that simply print hundreds (or thousands) of one-line facts, like:

The deepest spot on the ocean floor is known as Challenger Deep, which is 36,307 feet below the ocean's surface.

YAWN. But suppose I told you this:

The first people to attempt to measure this giant hole in the ocean, back in 1875, used a weighted rope that stretched down more than 26,000 feet.

What? Who has a rope that's FIVE MILES LONG? See, that kinda stuff is much more interesting.

So you will not get bland, one-line pieces of data with my books. I'd pass out from boredom putting them together, and I can only imagine how mind-numbing they'd be to read.

I like the little stories that go with the stuff labeled 'trivia.' Gives them substance. Provides some depth. And just makes them more interesting.

This book won't be for everyone. Nope. You might prefer endless lines of stats. Power to you. There are thousands to choose from. Happy trails to you.

But if you enjoy a bit more, then look at it this way: Those books are just French fries; this book is an order of fries with multiple dipping sauces.

And maybe even a chocolate shake. Let's dig in!

BBG

CONTENTS

1.	Chocolate	1
2.	Disneyland	7
3.	Top of the World	13
4.	Bottom of the World	19
5.	Elevators	25
6.	Anesthesia	31
7.	Pyramids	35
8.	Ants	41
9.	Traffic Lights	47
10.	Bacon	53
11.	Waterfalls	59
12.	Coffee	65
13.	Mosquitoes	71
14.	Doughnuts	77
15.	Convenience Stores	83
16.	Mail	89
17.	Bubble Gum	95
18.	Gambling	101
19.	Shoplifting	107
20.	Cereal Mascots	113
21.	Time Zones	119
22.	Flying Spiders	125
23.	Antarctica	129
24.	Commercials	135
25.	Electric Cars	141
26.	Buttons and Holes	147
27.	Money	153
28.	Mushrooms	159
29.	Mirrors	165
30.	Toothbrushes	171
31.	Trees and Rings	177

32. Bad Drivers	183
33. Witness Protection Program	187
Subscribe	193
More from Billy B. Good	195

Chocolate

Until the 16th century, chocolate was known only in Central America, where the cacao tree was a native plant. In fact, when Europeans got their first taste, they weren't exactly blown away by the chocolate drink they were given. Some referred to it as "a bitter drink for pigs."

I'd say we've come a long way.

In this chapter you'll learn:

- One country supplies nearly 40% of our chocolate
- The world's biggest chocoholics
- Could it help your love life?

Nobody knows for sure how long chocolate has been around, but new research suggests that it dates back more than 3,000 years. The Olmec society—in what we know today as the Veracruz and Tobasco regions of Mexico—figured out how to take the seeds of the cacao tree and manipulate them until they came up with a bitter, frothy beverage.

Yes, for millennia chocolate wasn't sweet, nor was it used as a food. It was a beverage that was treated as a divine gift. In fact, the Latin name for the cacao tree translates to "food of the gods."

The ancient Aztecs thought so highly of it that they used the cacao seeds as currency. They, along with the Mayans, also used chocolate as an integral part of many rituals and ceremonies. It's rumored that the iconic Aztec ruler, Montezuma, drank gallons of it a day.

It's unclear who first introduced the cacao seeds to Europeans. Some believe it was Montezuma himself, who mistook Spanish invaders for visiting deities and shared his special treat with them. Regardless, by the 1500s, cacao seeds had been shipped across the Atlantic. And, for centuries, it was a treat reserved only for the nobility of Europe.

In the early 1800s, a Dutch chemist figured out a way to cut the bitter taste and create a chocolate powder; it became known as Dutch cocoa. The next step was molding it into bars, a process that seems to have begun in the late 1840s.

By the end of that century companies like Cadbury and Nestlé (maybe you've heard of them?) had learned how to mass-produce a sweet version that became an international hit. The industry has never looked back.

And just how does it become the tasty treat we love? The cacao tree is a delicate creature, but after about 3 or 4 years each tree begins to produce football-shaped pods. (American football, by the way.) Once they're cracked open, about 40 or 50 cacao seeds spill out.

And get this: One tree's entire supply only yields about a pound of chocolate. So you need a LOT of trees.

The seeds are fermented, and that's where the distinctive flavor is born. Then comes the drying and roasting process. After that, workers open the shell and extract the bean guts, which are then crushed. The result turns into blocks of chocolate.

Trivia Snacks

Where do we get most of it today? About 70% of the world's chocolate comes from just four African countries. Yes, it has moved across the Atlantic.

Nigeria, Cameroon, Ivory Coast, and Ghana have the perfect hot, humid climate the plants love. Ivory Coast alone, in fact, with 6 million people working in the industry, supplies *more than 40%* of the chocolate you consume.

The vast majority of cacao beans around the world are produced on small, family-owned farms. The industry provides a livelihood for 50 million people. Sadly, the cost of processed chocolate in these countries means that most of the families harvesting the beans have never tried the finished product for themselves.

Who are the biggest chocoholics in the world? It's not even close. The Swiss, makers of delicious gourmet chocolate, consume an average of 20 pounds per person per year. Germany is next, at a little over 17 pounds.

Americans might think they have a sweet tooth, but they barely crack the top ten, devouring about 9 pounds per person each year. (Sounds like a good WEEK to me.)

How much cash does it pull in? Chocolate may not be used as currency these days, but it certainly generates a lot of cash. The global chocolate market (as of 2019) was about $130 billion per year, and it's expected to keep growing.

Do you crave it? There might be something wrong with you. Researchers say that continual chocolate cravings could be a sign that your body is not getting enough magnesium, a crucial mineral.

Yes, you can get it in chocolate, but it's best to get your magnesium from fish, nuts, seeds, beans, avocados, and spinach.

(Then have a little chocolate for dessert, right?)

Does chocolate affect your love life? Some of us refer to ourselves as chocolate lovers, but that might literally be true. The ancient Mayans certainly enjoyed their chocolate and referred to it as the "food of the gods." But the Mayans also were the first to associate chocolate as an aphrodisiac.

Today, claims regarding the cacao bean's effect on the human libido are continuously debated.

But, for what it's worth, chocolate *does* contain the chemicals phenylethylamine and serotonin, which are considered (by some) to be mild sexual enhancers. Others claim chocolate merely provides a placebo effect.

Hey, whatever works, pal.

Disneyland

An idea struck Walt Disney after he took his two daughters to an amusement park in Los Angeles. What if he could take the vision and feel that he incorporated into his movies, and build his own amusement park where parents and children could sense that same spirit? It took many years before his dream became a reality, but that dream also became a spectacular success.

In this chapter you'll learn:

- Thousands of people snuck in on opening day
- The park "employs" hundreds of real cats
- A popular junk food was inspired by Disney trash

By the late 1940s, Disney's movie studio was a hit, and people began writing and asking if they could visit. Walt Disney realized he didn't have a place that would actually entertain visitors. But he thought back to those early outings with his daughters, and by 1948 an official document—at the time labeled "Mickey Mouse Park"—showed up in the hands of Disney's studio production designer.

From there, the search for land was on. The company found and secured a 160-acre patch of land in Anaheim, California, covered in orange groves and walnut trees.

The biggest road block was money; Disney had the great idea, but not enough cash to finance the construction. So he entered a deal with ABC Television, and for the first five years the park would be owned by Disneyland, Inc, whose members included Disney, ABC-TV, and Western Publishing—the people who published the Little Golden Books. After those five years, Disney bought out all the shares and took full ownership.

On a Sunday in July 1955, Disneyland had a private opening for the media. And yet, more than 20,000 people showed up. Only half of those were actually invited; the rest either got hold of counterfeit tickets or simply climbed the fences and strolled around the new park.

Temperatures that day soared to over 100 degrees Fahrenheit, and making matters worse, a plumbers strike meant Disney had to choose between having working drinking fountains or working toilets. They chose toilets, which meant all the park's fountains were dry. This led to some scathing reviews; since Pepsi sponsored the park's opening, many thought it was a ploy to sell more sodas.

Legend has it that Walt's response was, "People can buy Pepsi-Cola, but they can't pee in the street."

Walt Disney wanted a hotel on site, but again was strapped for money. He approached the Hilton and Sheraton hotel companies, but they passed, saying they didn't even know where Anaheim was. (A decision I'm sure they're still kicking themselves over.) Disney eventually found a Texas oil millionaire to partner with, and the Disneyland Hotel opened three months after the park.

Within a year or two, the park's massive success caused other companies to quickly build all around the park. Soon, Disneyland found itself completely bracketed, which annoyed Walt. This was a major factor in his purchase of much more land in Florida for Walt Disney World.

Trivia Snacks

They built the park in a flash. Given just one year to get it done, the builders managed to meet the deadline—although not everything was finished or in perfect working condition on opening day.

Disneyland opened their gates with only 18 attractions, and 13 of those are still around today.

Wanna talk about realism? For the Pirates of the Caribbean ride, some of the props on opening day included real human skeletons, on loan from UCLA. Today, only one real human skull is part of the exhibit.

What did it cost for a ticket? In 1955, it was $1 for adults, and 50 cents for kids. The rides did cost extra, but only between 10 cents and 25 cents for children.

Today (as of 2021), a single day ticket for an adult begins at $104, and $98 for children.

Before COVID-19, it was only closed for three days: The day of mourning for John F. Kennedy, the Northridge Earthquake of 1994, and on September 11, 2001 (9/11).

It's home to a lot of feral cats. And that's by design. To this day, hundreds of them roam the park. Their job? Keep the population of rodents at bay.

The flags are fakes. The majority of U.S. flags flying above the park's buildings either have fewer than 50 stars or something off about the stripes. That way they're technically not legit flags and Disney doesn't need to perform proper flag protocols every day, such as lowering them at night or during bad weather.

There are no employees. That's because they must be referred to as cast members. And no "Mr." or "Mrs." Everyone is on a first-name basis, and that even included Walt, instead of "Mr. Disney."

Mind your piercings. For many years, facial hair was forbidden for cast members; today, it's allowed as long as it's neatly trimmed. Tattoos must be covered, and you cannot have any on your head, face, or neck. They limit piercings to the ears only, one earring on each side, and those must not be larger than a quarter.

When giving directions, cast members must use two fingers; using only one could be considered offensive in some cultures.

Plus, if working as a character (Pluto, Donald Duck, etc.), employees must learn how to properly sign that character's name.

Oh, and since this is SoCal, there are lots of movie celebrities walking around. But if a cast member asks for an autograph, that's grounds for termination.

The No-Fly Zone. No aircraft may fly within three miles of the park.

The No-Human-Remains Zone. Because there were so many reports of people spreading the ashes of departed loved ones on various rides, cremated remains are now on the list of banned items.

The birthplace of Doritos. A park restaurant called Casa de Fritos would repurpose old tortillas that otherwise would have to be discarded. They were nicknamed Doritos. In 1966, the Frito-Lay company decided the snack was good enough to sell nationally.

So your bag of Doritos was actually inspired by Disney trash.

Top of The World

Mount Everest formed about 50 million years ago when the Indian tectonic plate began banging up against the Eurasian tectonic plate. The result was the creation of the Himalayan mountain range and the Tibetan plateau. Today, Everest makes up part of the border of Nepal and the Tibet Autonomous Region of China.

In this chapter you'll learn:

- The mountain top sees traffic jams
- The original listing of its height was a lie
- Hundreds of bodies litter its slopes

The massive crunch of the two continental plates colliding resulted in some interesting geology. The summit of Mount Everest contains marine limestone, evidence that it once didn't sit on top of the world but rather lay beneath an ocean floor.

The name of the mountain depends on who you ask. It's called Chomolungma by the Tibetan people, while the government of Nepal named it Sagarmatha, which means "goddess of the sky."

In 1841, a British survey team happened upon the massive mountain. Sir George Everest led that team. At first they simply called the mountain Peak 15; then, in 1865, the western world began calling it Mount Everest.

Of course, when there's a mountain, there will be people who want to climb it.

Ever since the team of Tenzing Norgay and Sir Edmund Hillary reached the summit in 1953, climbing Mount Everest has represented the peak (ha!) of human achievement.

It's a crowded place. Once it became THE challenge—and a guarantee of winning every game of one-up at a bar—thousands have attempted to reach the top of the world.

An average year sees between 800 and 900 people grab their climbing shoes and bottles of oxygen and head up. That causes serious—and deadly—problems. There's photo evidence of traffic jams, dozens of people waiting in punishing weather conditions to scale the final few hundred feet.

Everest was declared the tallest mountain in the world in the 1850s. But deciding just *how* tall it is has always been difficult.

Early surveyors used trigonometry, relying on observations made from as far away as 150 miles. (The government of Nepal did not trust the British scientists enough to allow entry to their country to measure the mountain they deem sacred.) After years of working on it, Andrew Waugh announced that Everest was 29,002 feet above sea level.

But the story is classic. Waugh's calculations showed it was EXACTLY 29,000 feet . . . but he felt people would assume he just rounded his findings. So he added two feet, just so people would believe he hadn't fudged anything.

There's an old joke that Waugh was "the first person to put two feet on Mount Everest."

Today's estimates, using GPS, claim the summit is actually at 29,035 feet. However, different countries list different heights: Nepal says 29,028, while China prefers 29,015.

Those few dozen feet make little difference to your body, which would have complained long before you scaled to that altitude. Once you hit the 26,000-foot mark, you've officially entered what climbers call "the Death Zone."

That's why you see the poor slopes of Everest (and other peaks) littered with empty oxygen canisters. (Mountains are often a garbage-y mess.) But supplemental oxygen is critical. Of the roughly 5,000 people who've scaled Everest, fewer than 200 have succeeded without the extra air.

Oxygen deprivation not only saps your energy, it has killed hundreds (see below). Risks also include severe brain damage. And yet people continue to try.

Trivia Snacks

Everest is only the tallest when measured from sea level. The actual tallest mountain is Mauna Kea in Hawaii, at 33,500 feet—but most of that is below the ocean's surface.

Did you know Mount Everest is taller than it was a few years ago? It's grown about two feet in the last 16 years. Some experts say it's because of an earthquake in 2015 that shifted things a bit. Plus, the tectonic plate movement is still going on.

How's the weather? Cold and blustery. In fact, it's the winds that make it nearly impossible to climb over the span of several months. From November to February, it's not uncommon for wind speeds to reach 175 miles per hour. During most of the other months the wind will still howl at 100 mph.

There's generally a week to ten-day period in late May that provides a relatively safe window of opportunity, and that's when hundreds of people will rush to reach the summit, causing the traffic jams I mentioned.

It's not cheap to climb Mount Everest. Suppose you want to show off, or get the coolest social media photo EVER! Dude!

Well, you better save your pennies. And lots of 'em. These days the cost to visit Nepal and scale the mountain runs in the TENS of thousands of dollars. Some say as much as $60k-$100k.

Is it true there are still hundreds of bodies lying on the slopes? It's morbid to think about, but, sadly, it's true.

Along with the garbage and (ahem) human waste, around 200 bodies of climbers who perished dot the landscape. It's either too difficult to remove them, or they wished to be left behind.

That's tricky, because many of the residents of Nepal consider it an insult to leave corpses on the holy mountain. Plus, shifting and melting glaciers uncover some that were left decades ago.

Everest isn't even the most dangerous mountain to climb. Although opinions vary, some say it's only the *5th* most difficult.

So what claims the title as the most dangerous mountain? That would be the world's 10th-highest peak, Annapurna Massif, in Nepal. Forty percent of attempts to scale it have resulted in death. Whoa.

And why? Experts say it's a combination of the altitude, the terrain, and the always-horrible weather conditions.

Bottom of The World

Now that we've taken you to the top of the world, it's time to reverse course and head down. And I mean *way* down, to the deepest spot on Earth (we think).

In this chapter you'll learn:

- There's life down there
- The pressure is off the scale
- How long it would take a rock to sink to the bottom

We're piloting our boat off the coast of Guam to a spot just above a crescent-shaped gouge in the ocean floor. This scar along the bottom is called the Mariana Trench. It's an underwater canyon stretching five times the length of the Grand Canyon (about 1,600 miles), but it's only 43 miles wide.

Scientists are pretty sure this stretch of water contains some of the oldest seabed on Earth. Estimates put it at about 180 million years old.

And here's an odd fact: Although it's over 6,000 miles from the Mariana Trench to the United States coastline, it still falls under U.S. jurisdiction. Why? Because it's less than 200 miles off the coast of Guam, a U.S. territory. It's a maritime law thing.

So just how far below the surface are we talking? It plunges to about 36,200 feet. That's nearly seven miles below the waves.

And yet, as deep as the trench is, technically it's not the closest point to the center of the Earth. How can that be? Well, our planet bulges at the equator, kind of like a squashed tomato.

So, in order to get closer to the center of the Earth, you would need to sink to the bottom of a different body of water. And the icy depths of the Arctic Ocean's seabed holds that distinction.

Wait—there's *life* at the bottom of the Mariana Trench? What could possibly live down there?

Believe it or not, at pressures that would crush puny humans (more below), expeditions have uncovered life. And not just a stray creature or two; you'll find lots of it down there.

They're mostly single-celled organisms, called xenophyophones, but there are also larger critters, including amphipods (similar to shrimp) and sea cucumbers.

At the 26,000-foot depth a Mariana snailfish has been spotted, happily hunting in a zone where it has no competitors for food. Mud at the bottom has also revealed hundreds of other microorganisms, apparently feeding off the sulphur vents.

Many scientists back up the claim that we know more about the moon than we do about the ocean floor, and that includes the deepest points, such as the Mariana Trench.

The main reason for this has to do with light and radio waves. Although the moon is nearly a quarter of a million miles away, it's illuminated, so we can see it. The ocean's deepest areas are pitch black, and the sea water even interferes with radio waves.

So the best we can often hope for is using acoustic waves to monitor the echo off the seabed in order to map the terrain. The bottom of the world is simply dark and mysterious.

Trivia Snacks

Just how far down is the very bottom? To put 36,200 feet into real perspective, visualize this: At its deepest point, you could place Mount Everest inside the Mariana Trench and there would *still* be another mile before you reached the surface. How's that for perspective?

Or, if you'd like a moving image, consider this: You could lean over the edge of your boat, drop a rock into the water, and it would take well *over an hour* to sink to the bottom.

The pressure is mind boggling. To understand the amount of pressure you'd experience at the deepest part of the ocean, you need some reference. In this case, we'll use the classic jumbo jet.

When you go that deep, all those miles of water place a staggering amount of pressure on everything. Like more than *1,000 times* the pressure you'd feel at the surface. That's the equivalent of nearly 50 jumbo jets stacked on top of your head.

It's hot and it's cold. As you might expect, that far below the surface, where sunlight has no chance to penetrate, water temperatures will drop to between 34 and 39 degrees Fahrenheit. But wait—it gets hot, too. Thanks to a series of hydrothermal vents, there are places in the Trench where the temperature climbs to a scalding 700 degrees.

So how do we visit? Well, you probably never will. As of 2020, while 5,000 people have scaled Mount Everest, only *13* people have been to the deepest spot on Earth. That means it's quite possible that Mars will see its first 50 visitors before that number of people visit the bottom of our world.

I'm talking about the area of the Mariana Trench called Challenger Deep, named after the first ship to ever study this canyon in the 1800s, as well as the HMS Challenger II in the 1950s.

The first two people to descend in a bathyscaphe (a deep-sea submersible vessel) were U.S. Navy Lt. Don Walsh and Swiss oceanographer Jacques Piccard.

Fun trivia side note: Piccard's father once set a record for reaching the highest altitude in a balloon, so father and son had records for highest flight and deepest dive.

Who was brave enough to first try it alone? The first *solo* trip to Challenger Deep was undertaken by filmmaker James Cameron—the guy behind *Titanic, Avatar, The Terminator*—in 2012. Naturally, he made a pretty cool documentary out of it, called Deepsea Challenge. Check it out in IMAX format if you can.

The science of descending that deep is impressive. To get there, submersibles flood water tanks in order to drop. But once at the bottom, the pressure and freezing temperatures won't allow you to just disperse the sea water. So, in order to ascend, the craft will release ballast in the form of iron shot, which is left behind on the sea floor.

Elevators

How'd you like to ride in an elevator that travels so high, so quickly, that it was engineered to protect your ears from the rapid change in air pressure?

I'll tell you about it in a bit.

In this chapter you'll learn:

- Elevators led to penthouses
- The "Close Door" button is a joke
- Surviving the longest drop in history

How long have elevators been around? Technically, for over 2,200 years. Famous Greek mathematician Archimedes sketched a design for a man-powered lift.

Through the years these hoists were used to lift people, building materials, and livestock. There were two dozen elevators at the Roman Coliseum, powered by slaves.

Today's modern marvels are electrically powered, and first demonstrated in the 1800s. And yes, the Otis name you see on so many of them? That's the company launched by Elisha Otis, who showed off his design at the 1854 World's Fair in New York.

Elevators actually produced penthouses. How? Because before elevators were around, the top floors of buildings were reserved for servants. Wealthy, important people refused to walk up too many flights of stairs, so they forced their servants to trudge up there.

Ah, but with the invention of modern elevators, the big shots swapped places with the help.

And obviously there would be no skyscrapers without elevators. Few people would walk up 100 flights of stairs. Especially to go to work.

After reading this next segment you'll always have a good laugh when you watch someone impatiently punching the Close Door button.

Those don't do anything. They're essentially a placebo.

Why? Because people like to feel in control, and since there's a bit of anxiety associated with elevators anyway, designers gave you a little something to feel like you're controlling the machinery.

You're not. But have fun stabbing that button, anyway. Elevator designers are somewhere, snickering.

(Postscript: In New York City the law says those buttons *must* work—but they're on such a long delay that, when you get right down to it, they really don't.)

Next stop: Space! Rockets are expensive and suck down millions of pounds of rocket fuel. So engineers are hoping to someday build a space elevator. It would consist of a massive cable attached to the Earth, stretching to a geosynchronous-orbiting platform about 22,000 miles up.

The battle between Earth's gravity and the centrifugal force of the orbiting platform would create tension to keep the cable taut. Then you'd attach cargo cars and lift people or supplies up to space with no need for rockets.

Sounds really futuristic, right? Well, the idea was first suggested by a Russian scientist in 1895.

Trivia Snacks

How many people do elevators carry each day? They are the #1 form of transportation in the world, making a combined 325 million trips every day, traveling 1.3 billion miles per day. Experts say all these trips combine to carry over 2 billion people every 24 hours.

Are they dangerous? You could say they're the safest form of transportation on the planet. About 30 people per year die in elevator accidents—but about half of those are elevator technicians working on the machines.

Who survived the biggest drop? This is quite a story. In 1945, a 20-year-old elevator operator named Betty Lou Oliver was working in the Empire State Building. Her elevator was on the 80th floor when disaster struck.

Because of heavy fog, a B-25 bomber crashed into the building between the 78th and 80th floors. Betty Lou was injured and placed into another elevator to be lowered. But the airplane crash had damaged the cables, and, without warning, they gave way. She plummeted more than 75 floors to the basement. Although she survived, she suffered a broken pelvis, neck, and back. Newspaper accounts described her survival as a miracle.

How fast will they go? Remember the air pressure/ear issue I mentioned? That applies to a speedy elevator servicing a skyscraper in Guangzhou, China. It zips passengers from the 1st floor to the 95th in 42 seconds. That works out to about 45 miles per hour.

Engineers worked out a device to gradually adjust the air pressure in the car to help your ears equalize. Otherwise you'd be in some pretty serious pain.

Ever been trapped in one? The record for longest time spent trapped in an elevator (that we know of) belongs to a guy named Nicholas White. In 1999, he was working late on a Friday night when he took a smoke break. During his ride back to the 43rd floor, the elevator stopped between floors. And didn't move.

This was before many people had cell phones. And it was the weekend. Nicholas was in there for *41 HOURS*.

PS: He'd also been stuck in an elevator for 20 minutes when he was a kid. This guy needs to take a ground-floor job.

Superstition rules. Because of the fear of the number 13, many buildings skip over that and go from the 12th floor to the 14th. The Otis Elevator Company has estimated that fewer than 20% of their elevators have a button for 13.

And why do they have such horrible music? Through the years, the term 'elevator music' has picked up a pretty bad reputation. But it did serve a purpose when it was first suggested.

It was the 1920s, and most people had never experienced a modern elevator. So people were naturally nervous about it. Calming, soothing music was pumped into the cars, with the hope it would get people to relax. Who knew it would lead to such torture?

Anesthesia

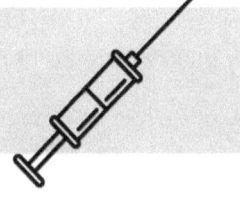

The clinical definition of anesthesia involves the "temporary loss of sensation or awareness," often for the sake of surgery or some other medical procedure. It can bring on unconsciousness, even amnesia, but ideally it'll spare you from pain.

In this chapter you'll discover:

- Early anesthesia involved wine
- Can you wake up during surgery?
- Why redheads might need more juice

One of the most interesting things about anesthesia is that we really have no idea how it works. We're just happy that it does.

Imagine the days BEFORE anesthesia. What did people do when they needed a surgical or dental procedure? Well, the short answer is: They suffered.

But history tells us there was experimentation with herbs. Then came the use of alcohol—so the best we could do, I guess, was get you drunk before cutting you open.

The ancient Egyptians may have used an extract of the mandrake fruit, and Chinese legend tells of a doctor named

Bian Que who allegedly performed a heart transplant in the 4th century BC after giving the patient an "intoxicating wine" that feigned death for a few days.

Okay, but when did we get the good stuff? It wasn't really that long ago. The first report of an inhaled anesthesia was in 1845. Horace Wells, a dentist, put on a demonstration of his "exhilarating gas." We know it today as nitrous oxide, which some people call laughing gas.

The demonstration, a tooth extraction, did not go well. Some reports say the patient cried out in pain during the procedure, so people in the crowd chalked it up as a failure.

Imagine being the first volunteers for that.

One of the most well-known anesthetics is ether, and we think it was being processed as far back as the 8th century. It still took a few centuries for people to figure out, *Hey, this stuff makes me feel funny!* A Swiss doctor and chemist named Paracelsus observed that chickens who were administered ether would either feel no pain, or simply fall asleep. Even with that flag waving in our faces, humans only used ether for the next couple hundred years as a recreational drug. Damned 18th century hippies!

All right, but how can we *not know* how anesthesia actually works? Well, there are *theories* about how it works, and a recent study suggests that it involves weakening the electrical signals between neurons.

Here's what makes it complicated: We didn't evolve to be impervious to pain. Pain is a warning signal to protect us from further harm, right? Touch the hot stove, it burns, you pull your hand away to prevent significant damage to your body. So shutting down your brain to cut open your body goes against our evolutionary progress.

The mystery of anesthesia is such an unknown that five different people can react in five different ways. Now you know why anesthesiologists go to school for a LONG time.

Trivia Snacks

How many surgical procedures are performed each day? In the U.S. there are a little over 50 million surgeries a year, which means around 135,000 every day.

Not all will use general anesthesia—which essentially puts you to sleep—but obviously most do.

Can people wake up in the middle of surgery? Okay, so it *does* happen. But rarely. Statistics show that about 1 or 2 people out of a thousand may experience a condition known as *unintended intra-operative awareness*.

Because their muscles are relaxed, however, they're unable to let the doctors know, "*Hey, I feel that!*"

Again, it's very rare. Probably shouldn't let that fear keep you from having the operation.

Why do they tell people to avoid food for several hours before they're anesthetized? Because general anesthesia will relax the muscles in your digestive system and airway. When that happens, it's possible for food and stomach acid to pass from your stomach into your lungs. And that's not good.

By fasting, you're helping to eliminate the possibility of anything making that trip.

But what if I'm a redhead? I heard that makes me more sensitive to pain and less likely for anesthesia to work.

Talk about a debate! And it's a debate that has carried on for decades. In a nutshell, the theory goes that a true redhead requires more anesthesia (general or local) than, say, a brunette or blonde.

It has to do with a connection between the cell receptors responsible for the pigment in hair and a hormone that controls pain sensitivity.

The sad offshoot of this theory (whether true or not) is that dentists claim redheads don't visit often enough out of fear the novocaine won't work on them.

You've heard the phrase "bite the bullet," right? That was once a solution for dealing with battlefield surgery. They'd give the patient a bullet and tell them to bite on it while they broke out the knives.

It was a different time.

Pyramids

They've captured our attention for thousands of years, and we marvel that they've survived for so long. But so much about the pyramids remains a mystery.

In this chapter you'll learn:

- One pyramid was the world's tallest building for 3,800 years
- What it would cost to build the Great Pyramid today
- The Great Pyramid is not the world's largest

There are way too many gaps in our knowledge of ancient pyramids. But we're fairly sure they were primarily built to be tombs for rulers and other VIPs. The ancient Egyptians believed that the soul, or essence, which they called *ka*, survived after death. That's why they went to such great lengths to care for the body, including the detailed preservation in the form of a mummy.

That's also why they supplied the tombs with so many objects that would serve the individual as they moved on in the afterlife: food, weapons, even boats for transportation.

Many experts believe there's an important connection between the construction of the pyramids and their alignment with certain stars. And some have suggested a strong correlation between the alignment of the three enormous pyramids on the Giza Plateau and the three primary stars that make up the belt of the constellation Orion.

You may have heard of The Seven Wonders of The Ancient World. The Great Pyramid on the Giza Plateau outside Cairo is the oldest—and only surviving—member of that famous collection.

Built for the ruler named Khufu (or Cheops, as the ancient Greeks called him), it's around 4,500 years old. And it held the title of tallest human-made structure in the world for 3,800 years, which is incredible. The Lincoln Cathedral in England finally surpassed it in the 14th century.

One funny side note about the Seven Wonders of the Ancient World: The original wording in Greek was meant to convey not wonders, but simply things that should be seen. Similar to today's lists of "Things to see before you die."

So the original listing of the Seven Wonders was actually more of a touristy guide book.

Thieves often raided pyramids. In fact, almost since the day they were completed, pyramids have been targets for people looking to get rich. Untold millions of dollars worth of treasure and artifacts have been lifted from the tombs.

Not only that, but the limestone coverings on the outside—which in their heyday made the pyramids glitter like jewels—were stripped and carted away.

Some will tell you that the Great Pyramid is the largest in the world. But it depends on *which* Great Pyramid you're referring to. There's the one in Egypt, and it's certainly the tallest in the world, rising 451 feet above the sand. Plus, keep in mind that it has eroded through the millennia; originally it stood about 30 feet taller.

If you're talking about the largest in *volume*, that would be the Great Pyramid of Cholula in Mexico. It may be less than half the height of its Egyptian cousin, but it dwarfs every other pyramid in volume, at almost 4.5 million cubic meters. That's because its base is four times larger than Egypt's Great Pyramid.

That also makes this Aztec temple the largest monument of any kind ever erected. It doesn't get as much attention, though, because it's covered in dirt and grass, and to the untrained eye it simply looks like a mountain. Even the Spanish explorers missed it. In fact, one of them built a church on top of it—a church that remains there today.

Trivia Snacks

Natural AC. The temperature inside the Great Pyramid is a constant 68 degrees Fahrenheit, no matter how hot it gets outside on the Giza Plateau (which can often climb to over 100 degrees).

How many blocks of stone went into the Great Pyramid in Egypt? More than 2.3 million of them. It's a number that's difficult for us to fathom.

And how large were these blocks? Some were more massive than others, but the average stone weighed about 2.5 tons.

So 2.3 million stone blocks, each weighing around 5,000 pounds. And remember, they had no modern machinery to lift them or shift them from place to place.

How many people worked on the Great Pyramid? Early estimates suggested about 100,000 people over a span of 20 years. However, recently the number of workers has been placed at around 20,000.

For centuries people believed they built it with slave labor. But that's been disputed, and many now assert that it was constructed by a paid labor force.

What would it cost to build today? That's hard to say, mostly because we're not sure *how* they built it so long ago. But, based on the plan we're most confident in (involving a spiraling ramp as they built it from the inside out), and even using modern cranes and other equipment, some estimate that it would cost nearly $6 billion.

How many people visit Egypt's Great Pyramid? In an average year, over 10 million people visit the pyramids in Egypt, and the tourism industry brings in more than $12 billion.

Ants

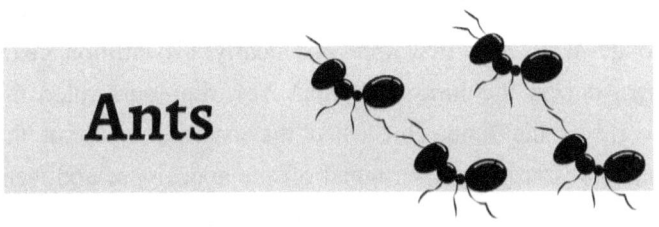

You see them outdoors, you occasionally find them wandering *inside* your house, and they pretty much make themselves at home wherever they like. Why? Because they've been here a lot longer than we have, and they put the adapt in adaptable.

In this chapter you'll learn:

- The numbers will boggle your mind
- They communicate with chemicals
- Their ancestors were enormous

We humans like to believe we're the dominant species, but ants might scoff. And honestly, they have a way stronger resumé than we do.

You'll find them on six of the seven continents, and who can blame them for ignoring Antarctica? They do a pretty good job of making themselves at home, whether or not they're native to an area.

Take Hawaii, for instance. Of the 50 or so known species there, not one is native to the islands. They're considered an invasive species, probably carried to the tropical paradise on our ships.

The little dudes have been around for a long time. How long? Well, ants first appeared nearly 170 million years ago, during the Jurassic Period. Yes, dinosaurs ruled the world at the time. But when the asteroid took out the terrible lizards, ants shrugged off the apocalypse and went about their business. That's mighty intimidating.

Let's talk about superorganisms. That's what ant colonies can become. Put 50 million of them together and they'll operate as a single unit. In order to make those kinds of numbers work, you gotta communicate. Entomologists (who study insects) and myrmecologists (who specifically study ants) are stunned by their abilities to communicate and cooperate.

The way they do it is fascinating. Ants communicate mostly through chemicals. They use pheromones for a variety of reasons, such as warning of danger, or spreading the news of a new discovery of food. Scientists say it's a quick and very efficient form of communication.

Their antennae are used to detect chemicals, air currents, and vibrations. They also receive and transmit signals through touch.

Trivia Snacks

How many ants are alive at any given time? Okay, get ready for a LARGE number. While there are 7 billion humans occupying the planet, estimates place the number of ants at between one and ten QUADRILLION.

A quadrillion is *a million billion*. Visually, ten quadrillion looks like this:

$$10,000,000,000,000,000.$$

They're not all tiny, either. Some ants, such as the giant Amazonian ants of South America, can grow to almost an inch and a half in length. But if that seems big, check this out: Fossils of prehistoric giant ants show these suckers grew to nearly *the size of hummingbirds*. How'd you like to find *that* crawling through your kitchen?

How many species are there? There's no way to accurately answer that, at least today. Right now we've catalogued about 12,500 different species. But some entomologists believe we may have discovered only *half* the species in the wild. There are a lot of ants still out there, undocumented.

How long do they live? There's a wide span here, ranging from weeks to months to years. There are a few, often the queens, who can live for decades. Yes, it's not uncommon for some queens to live as long as 30 years. The males, whose only job is to mate, generally last only a week. But what a week! (Sorry.)

They can be brutal. As you may have seen in nature videos, they go to war and they practice slavery. Ants do battle with neighboring colonies, and it's often vicious. They fight by either biting, stinging, or even spraying a form of acid on their opponents. Ants, in other words, do not fight fair.

And even without war, they're well known for capturing the eggs or larvae of their enemies and forcing the newborn ants into slavery, working for the conquering hive.

They can be really destructive to humans, too. One example? Fire ants cost Americans about $5 billion every year, from their stinging bite to the damage they cause to property.

Carpenter ants, contrary to popular belief, are not eating the wood in your house. What they are doing, however, is boring through your home to enlarge their nesting area. Pest control companies in many parts of the world make a substantial living fighting off this particular species.

What about the bite? Well, it could knock an MMA champion to their knees. The bite of a Bullet Ant—so named because victims say it feels like you've been shot—can inflict non-stop pain for as long as 24 hours.

At the same time, they're incredibly smart. Some experts who rate the intelligence of insects claim that ants are second only to honey bees in terms of their brain power. So show a little respect, will ya?

Are they edible? Some, yes. In some countries they're considered "insect caviar." There's a species known as the "big butt ant" that's especially popular in South America. Some say it tastes like buttered popcorn. And they hate the way they look in jeans.

Traffic Lights

They're so much a part of our everyday lives that we take traffic lights for granted. But they've come a long way, quickly.

The first one blew up. How's that for an ominous beginning?

In this chapter you'll learn:

- They used to be only two colors
- Why red works well with your brain
- How much time we spend waiting for lights to change

Wait, what was that part about the first one blowing up? See, the first traffic light was gas-powered, because this was December, 1868. They set it up outside Parliament, one of the busiest intersections in all of London, and a police officer ran it.

A pillar contained red and green gaslights, and the cop would manually adjust them according to traffic flow. Well, it only took about a month before something went wrong. On January 9th, 1869, a leak in one of the gas lines caused the thing to blow up, injuring the cop on duty.

Before we had electric traffic lights, we had panels that would drop down, with one saying Stop and the other Go, or sometimes Proceed. Kerosene lamps, using red and green tinted lenses, helped illuminate the signs at night.

In 1912, a policeman in Salt Lake City, Utah, developed the first traffic light powered by electricity. And in 1914, one was installed in Cleveland, Ohio. These early lights had only two colors, red and green. They were also paired with buzzers to indicate that the color was about to change. But eventually it became clear that it was downright dangerous to just switch from green to red. So another police officer came up with the idea for a yellow warning light. The first four-direction, three-color light that we recognize today was created in Detroit, Michigan in 1920.

Many of the earliest traffic lights had to be manually controlled. So somebody had to sit there and flick them from red to green and back again. Eventually, though, computers took over.

In the 1950s, the first computer-controlled lights were installed. And they were a big hit. Primarily because they allowed pressure plates to be installed at intersections. These plates told the computer that there was traffic waiting, which controlled the length of the red/green cycle.

Pressure plates also told computers how many cars were waiting, and that data helped to program the network of lights down a street.

For decades, the electric traffic light system used traditional light bulbs.

In the 21st century the switch to brighter, energy-efficient LED took off. But that introduced an additional problem. For years, the traditional lights got hot enough to melt accumulated snow. Since the LEDs run so much cooler, the snow sticks around.

Now engineers are placing heating elements on the lenses.

What's next? Well, engineers are developing a system for smart lights. They'll communicate with your car's navigation system to let you know how fast you should go in order to hit all the lights as they're green.

Other designers are looking into traffic lights that display news headlines within the red light, in order to keep drivers from being distracted by their phones and thus keeping their eyes on the light.

Trivia Snacks

Why red and green? Traffic lights for automobiles borrowed the colors used for years by train signals, although nobody really knows why those two colors were adopted to indicate go and stop.

But scientists say it worked out for the best. The color red has a longer wavelength, which means your brain can perceive it from farther away. And that means you have an extra fraction of a second to hit the brakes.

How long do we spend waiting at traffic lights? Hope you've got something good to listen to. In an average year, you'll spend about 58 hours waiting for the light to turn green.

Seems like longer in New Jersey. There's a traffic light in West Milford, NJ, that's been dubbed the longest red light in the world. If you get stuck there, you'll be waiting more than five minutes before it changes to green—and then it changes back to red after just a few seconds.

I'd seriously consider taking a different route.

Can't traffic lights be synchronized? The answer is yes, although many communities will tell you it's a very expensive process. However, some experts believe better synchronization between lights at various intersections could reduce traffic congestion by 10% and potentially reduce pollution by 20%.

Three-Two-One-GO! You've no doubt been sitting behind a driver who doesn't realize the light has changed from red to green, right? So you give the friendly two-tap on the horn. Well, some municipalities use a system known as a TSCT, or Traffic Signal Countdown Timer. It displays how many seconds are left before a light changes from green to red and vice versa. Studies show it can reduce the time that the first car waits once the light changes to green by as much as a full second, which adds up over multiple cycles.

However, some cities have removed the feature because too many drivers were using it like a drag racing countdown.

You can still see some of the oldest traffic lights. Take a trip to Asheville, Ohio, and you'll find a set of traffic lights that were installed in 1932. For being so old, they actually look kinda futuristic, described by some as "rocket-shaped."

And yes, size is everything. Originally, traffic lights were about eight inches in diameter. These days they're more likely to measure 12 inches.

However, some places around the world combine the two. The red light is 12 inches, while the yellow and green are only 8 inches across.

Bacon

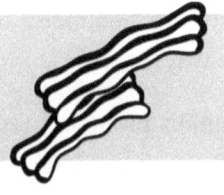

Love it or shun it, there's no denying the popularity for bacon. In fact, about 80% of people consumed the cured meat in the past year.

In this chapter you'll learn:

- The Spanish Johnny Appleseed of pigs
- Non-pork lovers find their own ways of having it
- How marketers created the bacon and egg sensation

It has recently exploded in popularity, but affection for bacon is thousands of years old. The ancient Chinese may be to blame for our addiction. They were curing pork with salt as early as 6,000 years ago.

But the taste caught on and spread west, until most of the Middle East and Europe were eating what they once referred to as *bacoun*, or as the Germans called it, *bakkon*.

At one point the word described *any* pork product, but by the 1600s it was exclusively used to identify the salted belly or sides of a pig.

Prior to the invention of refrigeration, salt-cured pork was purely a method of preserving food; but people developed a liking to the taste, and even after the advent of refrigerators we've continued to prepare these cuts of pork the same way.

Columbus brought a few pigs with him to the new world, but Spanish explorer Hernando de Soto has been called "The father of the American pork industry." It wasn't his intention; he simply arrived in what's now Florida in the 16th century with 13 pigs. That number soon swelled to 700, and before you knew it, wild pigs swarmed the country.

In fact, tens of thousands of pigs were still scooting around New York City as late as the mid-1800s. Yes, up and down the city streets. That prompted scoffs from visiting Europeans, but also concerns about health. It took the construction of Central Park before they gradually pushed the swine out of the city.

We're rebels. That's one explanation for the explosion in popularity of bacon. Some say it's a backlash—a piggish rebellion—against the movement encouraging healthy eating.

On the other side, though, vegetarians and vegans haven't completely ruled out the taste of bacon. Using marinated strips of soy protein, they have their own tasty snack. And some call it . . . *facon*.

Bacon made from mutton (sheep) has also carved out a decent market size, often referred to as macon.

There are many varieties of traditional bacon, too. Cuts vary, from side bacon which we get from pork belly, to back bacon taken from the loin in the middle of the back. Back bacon is the primary cut used in the U.K. and Ireland.

There's also collar bacon, cottage bacon, and something known as jowl bacon, which, yes, comes from the animal's cheeks. You first.

Trivia Snacks

Bacon is big business. How big? $59 billion every year. And industry folks say that'll creep up close to $70 billion in just a few years.

In the U.S. that translates to about 1.7 billion pounds consumed annually, and 70% of that is polished off at breakfast. The average person eats about 18 pounds of bacon every year.

How do you like it cooked? About 70% of people like it crispy, and 1% actually prefer it burnt.

It's a staple in a classic sandwich. Beginning in the early 1900s, people grew interested in this concoction known as the bacon, lettuce, and tomato sandwich. After World War II, however, it erupted in popularity, thanks to the sudden availability of the ingredients. Until recently, it was voted the #2 most popular sandwich in the U.S., and #1 in the U.K. However, its hold slipped, thanks to a surge in popularity of the grilled cheese sandwich.

How do the pigs keep up with all this production? The average hog produces about 15 pounds of bacon.

We practically worship it. Two-thirds of Americans say they'd be open to naming bacon the national food.

How did it get paired with eggs? Actually, that was a marketing ploy. In the 1920s, most people ate a light breakfast, often just coffee and maybe toast or a roll.

But a company hired to promote bacon convinced physicians to say that the body needed fuel to start its day. The advertisements recommended a dose of bacon and eggs—and they've been connected ever since.

Have you heard about bacon bombs? During World War II, people took their used bacon grease and returned it to their butcher. The butcher, in turn, donated the grease to the armed forces. And the military used it to make explosives.

You've probably heard the expression, "Bring home the bacon." But what does that even mean?

Well, it came from a town in England called Great Dunmow. Back in the 12th century, it didn't mean *bring home a big fat paycheck*. No, a church offered married men a side of bacon if they could swear before the rest of the congregation that they hadn't argued with their wife for a year and a day.

So a man who could *bring home the bacon* was held in high regard for both his good temper and his patience.

And finally, Edmund Bacon. He was a successful city planner, sometimes referred to as the Father of Modern Philadelphia, which got his picture on the cover of Time Magazine. That inspired one of his sons, who said, "I wanted to be more famous than him."

That son? Actor Kevin Bacon. I think he succeeded.

Waterfalls

We love them for their beauty, and we're in awe of their power. We even tap into that power to light up our cities and provide drinking water to millions.

In this chapter you'll learn:

- The largest waterfalls in the world
- Eventually waterfalls disappear
- How many people have gone over Niagara Falls in a barrel

Waterfalls can be broken down into as many as ten different types, depending on the various ways they descend. Besides the ones we're most familiar with, there are also many underground falls that have been discovered around the world.

Many of the world's waterfalls were created through the natural process of erosion, but some were also brought to life by the gouging of gigantic glaciers during ice ages. We can find one example of this in Yosemite Valley in California, where the Yosemite Upper Falls plummet more than 1,400 feet, thanks to a glacier's handiwork.

What's interesting is that nature doesn't really care for waterfalls, and over time will smooth them out. Through erosion, and over spans of thousands of years, a river will eventually carve its way out of a waterfall. The plunge pool at the bottom of the falls will lead to the collapse of the cliff itself and cause the waterfall to retreat. It's estimated that Niagara Falls has retreated about seven miles from where it originally began.

But this will happen to them all. The eye-popping, gorgeous waterfalls we see today will not survive Mother Nature over the long haul.

Whether they formed naturally or were artificially created, for years human beings have harnessed the incredible power of these wonders. The earliest known uses were to drive waterwheels, which helped with things like milling flour, grinding wood to use in making paper, and even to aid the manufacture of cloth.

In the modern era, waterfalls have become tremendous sources of hydroelectric power. The plunging water spins the blades of massive turbines, and the process generates electricity which is sent down transmission lines.

Hydropower is the most widely used form of renewable energy around the world. In many cases, dams are built to contain rivers or lakes, and the water gradually spills through a waterfall to drive the turbines.

Worldwide, about 1,300 gigawatts of energy is created through hydroelectric generators. The top producing countries are China, the United States, and Brazil.

Trivia Snacks

What's the largest waterfall in the world? Well, it depends. Are we talking about the tallest? That's Angel Falls in Venezuela, which plummets more than half a mile.

In fact, it's so tall that some of the water doesn't make it to the bottom. The long drop—and the air pressure—turns much of it into mist.

Okay, what about the widest? Now we're talking about the Khone Phapheng Falls in Laos, in Southeast Asia. Certainly not the tallest, but at their widest they stretch an astonishing 35,000 feet. That's almost seven miles!

Experts say the amount of water passing through these falls works out to about 410,000 cubic feet of water *every second*.

So Niagara Falls isn't that impressive? Sure, it's lovely. It's just not the largest. And it's still a remarkably popular destination for honeymooners and nature lovers. It's not unusual for the site to receive up to 30 million visitors a year, which in turn helps to employ over 40,000 people.

Water is big business.

Do people still go over Niagara Falls in a barrel?

Well, they shouldn't. More than 5,000 people have died trying. But the first person to try it in a barrel was a widowed teacher named Annie Edson Taylor.

In 1901, on her 63rd birthday, Annie took the plunge and survived. Bleeding, but alive.

What about the first man to survive it? His name was Bobby Leach, and about ten years after Annie, he rode in his custom-built metal barrel.

He also survived, but paid the price for his stunt: Bobby broke his jaw and both kneecaps and spent six months in the hospital. But he parlayed his experience into a publicity tour. Which didn't end well.

In 1926, Mr. Leach slipped on an orange peel and injured his leg, which developed gangrene . . . which killed him. Yes, he survived going over the falls in a barrel, but was doomed by an orange peel.

Waterfalls sometimes produce an interesting phenomenon of light called a moonbow. A moonbow is similar to a rainbow, but, as the name implies, it's created not from the light of the sun, but from moonlight.

Because the light source is so much fainter, the colors of a moonbow often are difficult to detect, and therefore it appears white.

Niagara Falls has been known to cast a moonbow, and the same is true for many others, including Cumberland Falls in Kentucky, the falls in Yosemite National Park in California, and on the Big Island of Hawaii.

Niagara Falls is turned off at night? Not exactly. But engineers on both the U.S. and Canadian sides do slow it down.

They divert water into reservoirs and use this downtime to check for damage, such as dangerous erosion.

The two countries also team up to make sure the falls don't freeze in the winter, which would hurt the electric generators.

Coffee

The origin of the world's 3rd most popular beverage (behind only water and tea) is shrouded in myths and legends. There's no definitive "first" associated with coffee, but we think it's been around for about 1,200 years.

In this chapter you'll learn:

- What country drinks the most
- What country produces the most
- How much it'll cost to open your own coffee shop

The first credible evidence of coffee consumption dates to the 15th century, when it was imported to Yemen from Ethiopia. Religious followers found it helped to keep them awake during late-night services, and it also staved off hunger during fasts. In fact, one possible origin of the word itself comes from the Arabic qahwah, from the verb qaha, which roughly translates to the phrase "to lack hunger."

Coffee made its way to Europe in 1565 when it arrived on Malta. Then, when merchants from North Africa began peddling it in Venice, one of the world's most influential ports, it spread like wildfire. At first, because of its rarity, it was limited to the wealthy who could afford it. By 1645,

Venice had the first coffee house outside the Ottoman Empire or Malta.

The first report of coffee in the Americas is in 1720, when seedlings were imported to Martinique in the Caribbean. Within 50 years, that small island had thousands of coffee trees.

What we call coffee beans are actually seeds. It takes about 3 to 4 years before a newly planted tree will produce viable seeds. From there, it takes multiple steps to process the seeds into the product you'd recognize today as a coffee beverage: Picking, drying, milling, roasting, and more.

The average coffee plant will produce about five pounds of green coffee beans each year, and those five pounds will result in less than one pound of finished product after roasting. Thank goodness the plants are hearty; the average coffee plant, if taken care of, will live about 40 or 50 years, but they've been known to last a century.

Trivia Snacks

Who drinks the most coffee in the world? I'd like to answer, "Mrs. Good."

But we're talking about countries, not an individual. And based on the statistics, the people in Finland must be buzzing!

In many countries, it seems there's a coffee shop on every corner. In Finland, they must have one in every room. The average person in this Scandinavian country consumes over 26 pounds of coffee per year.

Oh yeah? What about the United States? I mean, it seems like Americans are obsessed with the stuff, right?

Not even close to Finland. In fact, not even in the *top 20* around the world. As much as Americans love their lattes, espressos, or plain black java, they drink only a third as much as the Finnish. Works out to about 9.2 pounds per year.

That doesn't mean the majority of people don't enjoy it. Only 19% of adults in America *don't* drink this nectar of the gods, and about two-thirds enjoy it every single day.

Europeans are coffee freaks!

You have to scroll down to Number 10 on the list of coffee consumers before you'll find a country outside Europe.

That would be Canada. Folks in the Great White North gulp about 14 pounds of it each year.

How much do people spend on their coffee fix? (Maybe you should skip this section if you don't want to freak out a bit.)

The average American will drop about $1,100 every year on coffee. The numbers are even higher for 25 to 34-year-olds, where the annual expenditure on coffee is almost $2,700.

The truth is, about 40% of people admit they spend more each year on coffee than they invest in their retirement plan.

And it's not as if you can ignore the coffee shops. The United States has more than 35,000 of them. To put that in perspective, there are around 14,000 McDonalds and 25,000 Subway sandwich shops.

And 40% of the coffee shops in America have a Starbucks sign out front.

Wanna open your own cafe-style coffee shop? Research shows it'll cost you between $150,000 and $400,000 to get started.

Black? Or with cream? Turns out that one-third of people drink the stuff straight up, while the rest sweeten it with either milk, cream, or some sugary addition.

For latte lovers, the average number of add-ons (shots, pumps, syrups, etc) is two.

So we know who drinks it; who's actually producing it?

Brazil may not drink as much, but they sure do sell a bunch. In fact, the South American country is way out in front when it comes to peddling the bean.

How much? About 2.6 million metric tons of coffee beans every year.

The 2nd biggest producer is Vietnam, and then Colombia —which we'll always associate with the beverage.

Where did this stuff come from, anyway?

Once and for all: Is coffee good for you or not?

Ha! Did you say *once and for all*? Dream on! Experts will NEVER agree. But, as of 2020, some medical folks claim it could help prevent diabetes, Alzheimer's disease, and Parkinson's.

A post in the Harvard Health Blog touches on the potential of coffee to help reduce cardiovascular disease and certain cancers.

Many pediatricians, however, recommend that you don't start your child on their coffee journey until they're at least 12 years old. Has to do with the caffeine.

Please, consult your doctor.

Mosquitoes

According to estimates, wars throughout history have killed over 150 million people—and it could be much higher. But that's nothing compared to the most deadly killer on Earth: the mosquito.

In this chapter you'll learn:

- They're the biggest killer of all time
- They actually puncture you twice
- How many it would take to drain all your blood

Mosquitoes are considered one of a species of small flies; in fact, the word itself is from the Spanish or Portuguese for "little fly."

Even today, with modern medicine working hard, anywhere from 500,000 to two million people die every year from malaria that's transmitted by mosquitoes. Another 200 million to 300 million people are infected each year.

And that's just malaria. Mosquitoes also carry other deadly diseases, such as yellow fever and encephalitis. Some experts believe that throughout human history, nearly 5%

of all deaths have been related to a mosquito. That's a startling statistic.

Military historians will tell you that mosquitoes have affected the outcome of battles and entire wars, dating back to the Greco-Persian wars 2,500 years ago. Malaria devastated the Persian army, leading to a victory for the Greeks. Rome was both aided by and eventually a victim of the swampy, mosquito-laced Pontine Marshes.

But humans aren't their only targets. They're known to swarm around many other animals, including cattle. This can cause the cows to bunch together for safety, and that in turn will disrupt grazing, cause heat stress, and result in decreased milk production. Yes, all from mosquitoes.

Male mosquitoes generally live only a week, and females just a little longer. But that's all it takes for them to wreak havoc across the globe.

And what attracts them? It's different from person to person—some people are practically immune to bites, while they may cover the person beside them.

But scientists think most of the attraction comes from body chemicals, like the lactic acid in perspiration. They're also drawn to your exhaled carbon dioxide, and even to your movement.

When they do land on you, it's not just a single bite that you must endure. They'll actually stab you with *two* different tubes. One is used to inject some of their saliva, which acts as an anticoagulant to keep your blood from clotting. Yes, I know, it's gross. But that allows a smooth flow for them to ingest your tasty blood, which is done through the second tube.

But you should worry about that saliva, though, because *that's* what transmits the viruses and parasites they just picked up from their last victim. Wear your bug spray, my friend.

Trivia Snacks

Just how far will a mosquito travel in its short life? In that one week it could be as far as 20 miles. They prefer to fly into the wind in order to detect the odors that would attract them—but they also dislike strong winds. Those are the days when you're a little safer because they might hunker down.

How many species of mosquito are there? You'll find 174 different species in the United States, but worldwide there are around 3,000 different varieties.

Out of those 3,000, it's really only three that spread most of the deadly diseases around the world. Only one type carries malaria, for instance.

The female is prolific with her eggs. She'll lay about 300 eggs at a time, and she'll typically do that three times in her brief life. So figure nearly 1,000 little ones in one week.

They lay the eggs on the surface of water, which is why you'll find swarms of the little buggers near stagnant ponds and other water sources. The eggs hatch into larvae, which briefly feed on algae and other organic material. Not all survive, because they're vulnerable to hungry fish, dragonflies, and even ducks.

How many are alive on the planet at any given time? Hold on to your abacus: Experts believe there may be as many as 100 *trillion* mosquitoes buzzing around.

Who's out for your blood? While both males and females like the sugar found in plants, it's the female who's the real bloodsucker—she needs the protein in blood for her egg production.

Who are they most attracted to? Scientists say people with Type O blood are the most likely to be targeted. Mosquitoes also are attracted to your sweat, and to dark-colored clothing. If you have alcohol in your system, you're also a tastier treat.

Are these creatures doing any *good*? Yes. Each night, millions of mosquitoes are consumed by birds, bats, and frogs. They are most definitely an important part of the world's food chain. So as much as we want them gone, it would probably do much more harm than good.

In fact, some researchers are looking into ways of altering the genetic ability of mosquitoes to transmit diseases. So, instead of killing them off—and altering the world's food chain—we might be able to eliminate their disease-causing ability while leaving them around for other species to eat. All *we'd* be left with is the annoying itch, but no diseases.

A popular cocktail was created because of malaria. British soldiers in India in the 19th century disliked the taste of the medication used to treat mosquito-driven malaria. To mask the bitterness, they mixed it into a concoction of gin with water, sugar, and lime. And just like, the drink we know today as gin and tonic was born.

And one silly trivia snack for you: **How many mosquitoes would it take to bite you at one time in order to drain all of your blood?**

About 1.1 million of them.

I think you're safe. But what a great visual.

Doughnuts

It's surprising that we could fall in love with something originally known as "oily cakes." But it's safe to say that people are head over heels for their donuts.

In this chapter you'll learn:

- How donuts got their hole
- Donuts aren't the big money maker at donut shops
- How cops and donuts hooked up

It doesn't seem like a complicated invention, but how exactly did we end up with donuts? Well, we can thank the Dutch and the Native Americans. Archaeologists found petrified remnants of round cakes—with holes in the middle—in the ruins of Native Americans. They're perhaps the earliest known doughnuts in North America.

But the Dutch brought their own version to New York City. They called the treats olykoeks, but we 'Americanized' that to *oily cakes*. The Dutch fried their doughy creations in pork fat.

How did we get from Oily Cake to Doughnut? Legend has it that the mother of a 19th century ship's captain would make him circular fried dough. But the center wouldn't cook very well. So she filled that space with assorted foods like hazelnuts and found herself with a combo of dough and nuts.

Some say this is merely a romanticized version, and that the answer is much simpler: That bakers were asked to roll out "little nuts of dough" before frying them.

Well, is it *doughnut* or *donut*? The correct answer is: Either. Both are considered acceptable. But *doughnut* is the older cousin, with the first mention showing up in the early 1800s.

And the hole? How did that come about?

The real answer may be lost in the mists of time, and what we're left with is legend. However, that same ship's captain we met above—his name was Captain Gregory, by the way—allegedly shoved one of his mom's pastries onto the spokes of his ship's big steering wheel while he piloted it.

He liked that so much he instructed the ship's cook to just go ahead and make them with holes in the middle so they'd fit on the spindle.

There's also a legend that our same Captain Gregory didn't LIKE nuts, so he punched the center out of his pastry.

So how did we go from a few homemade delights to the bustling business we see today? We can thank a Russian refugee. Adolph Levitt, a baker in New York City, developed the first machine to mass-produce donuts in 1920.

Within ten years his machines cranked out millions of the tasty treats across the country, and Adolph was rolling in dough, literally and figuratively. While his machines spit out the donuts, the income from selling the mechanical contraptions to other bakeries was *really* lucrative; it brought him about $25 million a year.

During World War I, donuts were part of the plan to boost the spirits of soldiers battling through horrific conditions on the front line. Salvation Army officers Helen Purviance and Margaret Sheldon actually donned gas masks and carried pistols as they made their way through the trenches, bringing donuts and coffee to weary soldiers.

The gesture wasn't lost on the grateful soldiers. When they returned home after the war, they fueled a national surge in donut sales.

Then, twenty years later, the Red Cross took up the cause, and their Donut Dollies criss-crossed Europe in special vehicles fitted with giant vats for frying up fresh donuts for the front lines.

Trivia Snacks

Just how many do we consume? Hoo boy, I'm surprised we can fit into pants at all. Americans wolf down 10 BILLION donuts a year.

There are over 25,000 donut shops across the country. That equates to a $7 billion industry in the U.S. alone.

(Although, side note: Donut shops often make *much* more from their coffee than their cakes; some analysts think as much as 95% of their profits come from the java.)

There aren't as many people in Canada, but folks in the Great White North are #1 when it comes to donut shops per capita.

Medicinal donuts? Well, they tried, anyway. A donut shop in Portland, Oregon, dipped some of their treats into Pepto Bismol and then coated the donuts with Tums. The idea was that it was a donut for people who'd eaten too many donuts. Cute and clever; but the Food and Drug Administration wasn't laughing. They shut it down.

Never doubt the power of donuts to pack on pounds. While preparing to film the sequel to her hit movie *Bridget Jones's Diary*, actress Renée Zellweger needed to go from a size 6 to a size 14 in six weeks. Her eating regimen allegedly included 20 donuts a day. (Sounds heavenly, doesn't it?)

What about cops and donuts? Is there another profession that is more closely associated with a particular food? And how was this stereotype born?

In the 1950s, donut shops were some of the only places open during overnight hours. Police officers would stop in to grab an inexpensive pick-me-up during their shift. It also gave them a place to comfortably fill out their paperwork.

Plus, donut shops loved it because the employees felt much safer having the law around during those late shifts.

Convenience Stores

It's an industry that generates 3% of the entire gross domestic product sales in the United States. But so much of its history is built upon accidental discoveries.

In this chapter you'll learn:

- How a college football game changed everything
- The gift created by interstate highways
- How a broken soda machine led to an icy invention

The convenience store business model began simply enough, primarily because, at the time, there weren't really refrigerators like we know them today. In the 1920s, people picked up blocks of ice to tote home in order to keep their food chilled. Instead of today's computerized wonders of storage, people used literal iceboxes.

A man named Jefferson Green ran the Southland Ice Dock in Dallas, Texas. He sold these large blocks of ice to consumers, but in 1927 he had a random idea: Since folks are walking in to get ice, why not sell 'em some eggs, milk, and bread while we're at it?

His new store became a hit. They called it—and the others it spawned—Tote'm Stores. That is, until 1946, when they renamed them 7-Eleven.

Did they choose the name because of their hours? Actually, yes. Since practically every grocery store was closed and dark by the evening hours, 7-Eleven decided to stay open from 7 a.m. until 11 p.m. There was no real competition, and they had these evening and night hours to themselves.

As for eventually staying open 24 hours? It was purely an accident. After a University of Texas football game in 1963, the nearby 7-Eleven in Austin was packed with people. For HOURS. They couldn't close and stayed open all night. Later that year, 7-Eleven introduced its first *intentional* 24-hour location in (naturally) Las Vegas.

Then the Interstate Highway system inadvertently spawned an explosion of stores. It was 1956, and the Federal Highway Act meant over 40,000 miles of new roads and highways would be built.

Well, all those new highways meant a big need for fuel and rest stops. So just like that, convenience stores began opening like crazy around the country, providing both car and human fuel.

Another game-changer for the industry was the sale of beer and wine. Each state and county has its own laws regarding alcohol sales, but where it's legal those sales numbers were growing. So, one by one, convenience stores muscled their way into that segment, resulting in millions of dollars in increased revenue.

One convenience store ditched its car wash and replaced it with a wine store. At first some people complained; but I'd say the idea worked. The wine department now accounts for almost 30% of the store's sales.

Fill 'er up! The fuel crisis of the 1970s showed convenience store owners that gasoline could be a profitable line item. Keep in mind that in the early days, convenience stores were simply stores; they didn't sell gasoline.

But all it took were a few stores experimenting with it to show what a windfall it could produce. Soon, thousands of them installed pumps, which turned the gasoline industry upside down. Today, convenience stores around the U.S. account for about *80%* of all gasoline sales.

And obviously the oil and gas companies took notice. That's why you'll find Shell, Conoco, BP, and other convenience stores scattered around the world.

Trivia Snacks

How many are there? From that one humble ice store in Dallas, convenience stores quickly became a big hit. Today there are over 150,000 of them in the U.S. alone, and hundreds of thousands more around the globe.

How many people work there? It's estimated that 2.2 million Americans work in the U.S. convenience store industry, conducting more than 160 million transactions a day. And a survey in 2014 found that one in nine people worked at a convenience store at some point in their lives.

Coffee is a big reason for the success. Convenience stores in the U.S. sell an estimated 11 million cups of coffee every day. The java alone makes up about a third of their entire sales. (Some have joked that the entire industry could almost survive selling only gasoline, beer, and coffee.)

On the other end of the spectrum—from hot to cold—you'll find an icy hit. And, once again, it was entirely accidental. A man named Omar Knedlik discovered the soda machine at his Dairy Queen had stopped working. So he monkeyed around with some old automobile air conditioning parts and found it did a pretty good job—although what came out was more like a slushy concoction than a traditional soda. Omar didn't scrap it and start over; he cashed in on it.

His invention, at first called the Icee, was licensed by the 7-Eleven people, and sold as Slurpees. Sadly, Knedlik and his heirs didn't reap any long-term rewards from his discovery; he only made money from his licensing deal for 17 years—until his patents on the original Icee machine expired.

Today, more than 13 million are consumed every *month*.

Ever suffered from *sphenopalatine ganglioneuralgia*? Of course you have. But you've called it "brain freeze."

Well, the term was coined by the 7-Eleven people to describe the sensation when you suck down a Slurpee too fast. They've even trademarked the phrase, so don't even think of putting it on a T-shirt.

Mail

Even though we seem to rely on electronic communication these days (email, texts, social), people still put stamps on envelopes and shove them into a mailbox. And there are plenty of people whose job is to make sure it arrives at its destination.

In this chapter you'll learn:

- Robots can read your horrible handwriting
- What's the most valuable stamp ever?
- Mailing people is frowned upon—but done

If you were worried about the rise of the machines, stay out of your local post office. Because machines are doing the vast majority of the sorting.

Back in the day, a human being would sit in front of a conveyor belt and help sort mail that came in. The person would have to arrange the letter in the right direction (postage stamp on the top right), cancel the postage (so the stamp can't be reused), and then mark it for its next stop.

Not anymore. Today a machine does all of these steps.

Wait—the machine can read my handwriting? Believe it or not, yes. It's known as Optical Character Recognition

(OCR), and these suckers are really good at it. The machines can read typed text and even handwritten gibberish.

Unless it's TOO gibberish-y. Then the letter is kicked out of the system and sent to a human being to try to decipher. (Please, people: Penmanship.)

But this is actually quite rare. And you probably have similar capabilities on your computer and didn't know it.

The zip code helps with all this. Ah, but it's more complicated than you think. You may be used to simple five-digit zip codes, or possibly nine. But when the machine reads your letter's address, it actually sprays its own coding onto the envelope.

And that code could have as many as 19 characters on it. These detailed instructions can pinpoint not only the city and state, but the neighborhood, and sometimes even your specific house.

Yeah. The machines are pretty darned smart.

It's a common misconception that taxes pay for the postal service. But the USPS receives no direct funding from taxes. It's all supported by the sale of postage and products. Congress does, however, control the purse strings of the organization.

Trivia Snacks

How many letters and packages a day are processed? The numbers are staggering. Just using the United States as an example, every day (as of 2020) the USPS handles 182 million pieces of mail. Yes, every day. That works out to more than 5,000 every second.

They use almost a quarter-of-a-million vehicles to deliver the mail. And they actually work with private companies like FedEx and UPS. Those guys pay the postal service to deliver some of their packages, and the USPS pays the private guys for air transportation.

What's the most valuable stamp of all time? People have been studying and collecting stamps—a hobby also known as philately—for nearly 200 years. What's funny is that, at the time they were first used, nobody had any idea that these little items attached to envelopes would someday be worth (potentially) millions of dollars.

For now, the most valuable stamp is one created in the British colony of Guiana back in 1856. Known as the 1-cent Magenta, one of these black-on-red stamps was auctioned at Sotheby's in 2014 for nearly $9.5 million.

In the U.S., the legendary upside-down airplane stamp from 1918—officially known as the Inverted Jenny, and one of the most famous errors in stamp history—traded in a lot of four in 2019 for about $1.7 million.

How much mail is lost each year? To be fair, there's no real way of knowing this. One source cites a figure of 3%, but that's an estimate. The U.S. Postal Service does say that about 4.7% of mail is "undeliverable."

You've probably heard of cards and letters getting lost for years; so what's the record for the longest delay?

The Guinness World Record folks say it's 89 years, and happened in the U.K. Someone's RSVP for a Boxing Day party was mailed on November 29, 1919, and arrived at Weymouth, Dorset in 2008. The Royal Mail could offer no explanation for where the letter was for nine decades.

Can you mail a person? Okay, let's be clear: You should never try to mail a human being. It's illegal.

Well, it is *now*. Back in 1914, however, a family mailed their daughter between two towns in Idaho. They put her on a mail train with 53-cents in stamps attached to her coat. They said it was cheaper than buying a passenger ticket. And she made it to Grandma's house just fine.

A 19-year-old guy from the U.K. was working in Australia back in 1965 when he got homesick. He couldn't afford a ticket home, so he got two buddies to mail him home in a wooden crate. But not everything went according to plan.

He remained in the crate for five days, often losing consciousness, until someone peeked through a hole in the crate and saw him. The best part? He was in Los Angeles at the time; they had shipped him to the wrong place.

In the U.S., Congress passed a law in 1920 outlawing the mailing of human beings. That didn't stop a guy in Louisiana in 2006, and this is probably the best story of all. He was a prison inmate who broke out by climbing into a crate and actually mailing himself to freedom.

It worked. Temporarily. He managed to remain free for 18 months until authorities captured him again in Canada. As of 2020, he's confined to the supermax prison in Colorado, known as the "Alcatraz of the Rockies."

And probably kept as far from the prison's mail center as possible.

Bubble Gum

If you're a parent or grandparent, you've probably been hounded by little tykes whose eyes light up when they see a colorful gumball machine. That particular invention has quite the interesting history.

In this chapter you'll learn:

- The Mayans and Aztecs made theirs from tree sap
- An accountant invented our modern version
- The original recipe got lost

It's been a fun treat for kids and adults alike for nearly a century, but the man who's credited with creating it never made a cent in royalties.

Before we jump to the bubble version, though, let's see where chewing gum itself came from. It's actually been around for thousands of years . . . just not in the form we know it today.

Ancient civilizations chewed either resin made from tree sap, or a sort of tar made from the bark. In fact, people have had this oral fixation for at least 9,000 years. Back then, it was mostly used to clean teeth or to occasionally provide fresher breath. Some experts believe it could've been an attempt to relieve a toothache.

Both the ancient Mayans and Aztecs had their versions, too. They would collect a type of sap, known as chicle (chee-clay), which roughly translates to "sticky stuff," from sapodilla trees.

The modern version of chewing gum we know today was introduced and first sold commercially in the U.S. in 1848. William Wrigley, whose company focused on baking soda and soap, launched a brand of chewing gum in 1891. And I'd say he did pretty well for himself.

Ah, but let's get to the fun stuff. The bubbles!

The founder of the Fleer company (which later became known for its sports trading cards) attempted to create a chewing gum that could produce bubbles, but couldn't get it right.

The owner, Frank Fleer, messed around with a product he called Blibber Blubber in the early 1900s, but the texture was more like Silly Putty. He essentially gave up.

Then, in 1926, one of Fleer's company accountants, Walter Diemer, came forward with a recipe. Diemer liked to tinker with new gum recipes as a side-hustle, and he stumbled across a winner.

Fleer marketed this new treat as Dubble Bubble, and Diemer would actually train the company's salespeople on how to blow a bubble so they could demonstrate it in stores.

In the first year of production, Fleer sold $1.5 million worth of bubble gum . . . at one penny a piece.

There's a funny story about Diemer's first attempt at bubble gum. He was obviously excited when he came across a formula for gum that wasn't as sticky as normal gum and could stretch.

Except Walter somehow *lost his recipe*. It took him months to recreate it.

And here's one more fun fact about the great Mr. Diemer: Even though he came up with the winning formula, he never patented his bubble gum invention.

Today, nearly a century after he first showed his boss, sales have been in the billions of dollars. But Diemer didn't seem to mind. He continued working with the company for another 44 years.

Trivia Snacks

You might've noticed that most brands of bubble gum are pink. That's because when Diemer came up with his formula, it came out as a nasty-looking grey. There was only one food coloring available in the factory, which was red. When diluted, it came out as pink.

Bubble gum used to have a big drawback: It would stick to your face when the bubble popped. But companies worked on the problem, and by the 1970s had created a new formula that was synthetic. Ooh, even sounds tasty, doesn't it?

This new iteration became the norm, and soon people could pop without fear.

As of this writing, Chad Fell holds the world record for the largest bubble without the use of hands. Using three pieces of Dubble Bubble, his masterpiece measured about 20 inches in diameter. That's more than twice the size of an NBA basketball.

Susan Williams set the overall record. She produced a bubble measuring 23 inches across. She claimed to have produced a 26-incher during practice.

She also ran into a bit of trouble. She actually went on trial for refusing to stop popping her gum in the hallway of a courthouse where a murder trial was taking place. They charged her with disturbing a court proceeding. Witnesses said the gum-popping sounded like a pistol going off.

In an average year, about 100,000 tons of bubble gum are chewed around the world. It used to all head straight into landfills. But there are companies today that collect used gum and recycle it to make toys, containers, and other products.

Sorry to break it to you, Mom. If you swallow your gum, it will not stay in your stomach for seven years. It's true that your body has no interest in breaking it down quite like it does other foods. But bubble gum will work its way through your digestive system and come out you-know-where.

Gambling

Wherever you find a group of people gathered for an event—practically *any* event—you can rest assured someone will come up with a way to gamble on it.

In this chapter you'll learn:

- How much money people wager each year
- How gambling is similar to binge eating
- The remarkable story of the largest bet ever placed

Gambling has captivated us for thousands of years. So who were the first people to do it?

There are clues suggesting we've been gambling since before recorded history, as far back as the Paleolithic Age (commonly called the Stone Age). And several thousand years ago the Chinese may have used tiles for both games and lotteries.

The ancient Egyptians played a game called *senet*. And the oldest known examples of today's dice were used in Iran at least 4,500 years ago.

And people bet on everything? It's safe to say yes.

Sports, obviously. Lotteries. Animal races. The gender of the next royal baby. The winner of an Academy Award. When a celebrity gets married, you're able to gamble on how long it lasts.

There are some who insist that insurance is nothing more than another form of gambling. You're paying someone for car insurance, and they're essentially gambling that you won't have an accident.

Obviously it's big business when it comes to sports. You've seen it before: Team A is favored by four points over Team B. Contrary to popular belief, the number isn't a declaration of how much better one team is.

It's based on data, and meant for one purpose: To drive betting action. That's why the line changes as bets are placed. As more wagers are placed on Team A, the line increases, encouraging more people to bet on Team B.

As you can imagine, casinos rely on linemakers to keep things balanced and profitable.

Trivia Snacks

How much money is wagered each year? Well, the numbers are big enough that we might be able to say that gambling is truly America's (and maybe the world's) favorite pastime.

As of 2019, the industry contributed almost $140 billion to the nation's economy, and employed about three-quarters of a million people. Worldwide, it's estimated to be worth around half-a-*trillion* dollars to the economy.

Is it legal or not? Well, depends on what kind of gambling, and where you are.

In the early 20th century it was, for all intents and purposes, illegal just about everywhere in America. But gaming laws have become much more relaxed. If you count lotteries (and why wouldn't you?) gambling is sanctioned in 48 of the 50 states. The exceptions are Hawaii and Utah.

As of 2020, only Nevada and Louisiana allow casino gambling statewide. In 23 other states, it's restricted to certain areas. In some areas, for instance, it's limited to riverboats.

Let's talk odds. In a game of Texas hold 'em, the number of distinct seven-card hands is 133,784,560. And here's something you might find interesting: The probably of having NO pairs is actually less than the probability of having either a one-pair or two-pair hand.

The Gambler's Fallacy. That's an actual term, meaning the false notion that independent events of chance must somehow even out. An infamous game of roulette drove the point home.

It was August of 1913 in Monte Carlo, and the roulette ball fell on black *26 times in a row*. Gamblers lost millions, convinced that things had to even out and it MUST land on red. Nope.

Pinball wizards, rejoice. The city of Oakland, California, just lifted a ban on pinball machines in 2014. They'd been outlawed since 1930—because they were considered a form of gambling. Yes, pinball.

What sports generate the most money in gambling? People in the U.S. would love to believe that it's American football. But that's actually third worldwide, even though it generates billions of dollars annually. The original football—what Americans call soccer—is number one, followed by tennis. In fourth place, it's horse racing, then basketball.

Some experts believe that the *most difficult* sport upon which to gamble might be baseball. Why? Because of the unpredictability factor, with teams and individual players going through multiple hot and cold streaks.

What was the largest bet ever placed? This is tricky, because casinos are reluctant to release too much information—and for good reason. But there is the legendary story of the Phantom Gambler.

In 1980, he walked into Binion's Horseshoe Casino in Las Vegas carrying a suitcase with $770,000 (the equivalent of $2.6 million in 2021). He placed all of it on a single roll of the dice. And he won. He quietly took his winnings, now in *two* suitcases, and walked back out. They later identified the Phantom Gambler as William Lee Bergstrom.

He did the same thing four years later, this time walking in, putting down $538,000 ($1.8 million today) on one solitary roll of dice. And he won *again*. Then walked right back out.

The next time he tried this, just a few months later, he bet $1 million—and lost. This time he stopped afterwards, long enough to eat an enchilada. Then left.

Sadly, a few months after this, Bergstrom took his own life. His family later revealed that he was never a big gambler, and nobody was exactly sure why he made these three massive bets. Perhaps, they surmised, it was simply something he could be remembered for. Like I'm doing right here.

Is it true professional sports are allowed to rig games? Okay, it depends on your interpretation. In terms of gambling, absolutely not.

But sports leagues are allowed to "manipulate" the rules or adjust procedures in order to maximize consumer interest. For example, if one team is dominating through a particular style of play, referees can be "encouraged" to call more penalties or fouls for that specific play. That's documented, and no federal law prohibits leagues from doing it.

It's all about keeping spectators interested and the money flowing in.

How is a gambling addiction similar to binge eating? We sometimes consider both in the same family of what's known as process addictions, which also includes shopping, having sex, and gaming. They all can involve impaired judgment and trouble with impulse control.

For the record, if you think you may have a gambling addiction, there are services in many countries that can help. In the U.S., the number is 800-662-HELP.

Shoplifting

When I was 11 years old, I watched my friend sneak a Milky Way candy bar out of a store. I was mortified, and was sure I'd be going off to prison just by associating with the petty thief. Turns out my delinquent friend has a lot of company.

In this chapter you'll learn:

- It's rarely planned
- People used to be hanged for it
- The sticky fingers often belong to the store's employees

It's been suggested that shoplifting is the most common crime in America, and that may be the case around the world, too. Many countries and states lump shoplifting into the general category of larceny—the unlawful taking of personal property from a person or business—while others have specific laws laid out in relation to shoplifting.

What we know for sure is that the world is populated with a lot of sticky fingers. And yet there's no real profile of a shoplifter.

Demographics basically don't matter. Men and women shoplift equally. It happens in all age groups—although, contrary to popular belief, adults are more likely to do it than children.

The "five finger discount" isn't the domain of the poor and uneducated, either. A university study found that people with higher education and higher income were actually more likely to shoplift.

Scientists say this data suggests it's not financially motivated, but rather a psychological issue. It may be an outlet for anger, loss, depression, or feelings of disempowerment. Many psychologists say it can become an addiction. In fact, more than half of adult shoplifters say they began doing it while in their teens.

It's usually not premeditated. Three out of every four instances of shoplifting are spur-of-the-moment decisions.

When it comes to teenage shoplifters, nearly 70% say they certainly didn't need the items they took; they claimed it was an adrenaline rush that prompted them to do it.

And what's this? People used to be *executed* for it? Indeed. In England, the Shoplifting Act of 1699 made the crime punishable by death if the stolen item was worth more than five shillings. It's true that juries often chose to banish convicted shoplifters to either the American colonies or to Australia—but there were definitely hangings.

The last shoplifter to be executed in England was in 1822. Ten years later the law was changed to make it a non-capital crime.

Trivia Snacks

How many people are guilty? Some studies have said the number is about one in eleven, meaning tens of millions of people in the U.S. alone.

But in a survey in 2020, one in four adults admitted they had shoplifted at least once in their life.

Ah, but then there's the matter of getting caught. Experts believe that only one in every 48 shoplifters is caught, and even then only about half of those people are turned over to the authorities.

Some people shrug this off and say it's just a "cost of doing business." Don't kid yourself; companies most definitely factor this in when setting their prices, which means every time someone shoplifts, you essentially pay for it. Plus, when you factor in the cost from extra security measures, police time, the added burden to the court systems—well, it all adds up a great deal.

And how often does it happen? Across the country, retail estimates place the number at about 50,000 incidents PER HOUR. About ten million people per year are caught. In the time it takes you to read this one chapter, more than 1,000 items will have been shoplifted.

Another interesting element? Many shoplifters do actually buy one thing while stealing another in the same store visit.

What's the cost to businesses and the public? Estimates place the number at between $15-20 billion annually in the United States. Your average shoplifter might take anywhere from between $2 and $200 in merchandise per theft.

The National Association for Shoplifting Prevention—yes, there is indeed such a group—claims that $35 million worth of goods are lifted each and every day.

Of all the losses that stores experience, shoplifting accounts for about a third. Interestingly, another third comes from employee theft. The American Society of Employers claims that 20% of every dollar earned by companies is lost to employee theft. Sheesh.

What items are most-often shoplifted? Studies vary widely on this, but common items include meat, cosmetics, electronics, cigarettes, and pain relievers.

Oh, and pregnancy tests.

Books, too? Yep. Psychologists say it's often part of a condition known as bibliomania, which is the compulsive need to own and collect lots of books. Both libraries and bookstores report losses, but bookstores say it goes beyond that; they even have things like plants stolen, along with pictures off the wall.

The most common library books stolen are books on sex, prep materials for GED exams, and books on the occult and witchcraft.

The most well-known book thief was caught in 1990 after stealing over 23,000 books from libraries and museums in 45 different states and 2 Canadian provinces. They sentenced him to 71 months in prison.

Please, do not steal this book.

Cereal Mascots

You thought they just showed up one day and began peddling breakfast foods. But no; massive amounts of money went into their creation and their marketing. Today? They've been mostly gagged.

In this chapter you'll learn:

- How Snap, Crackle, and Pop used to have a buddy
- The Cap'N might not be a captain
- Tony the Tiger had to beat out a kangaroo

We know Snap, we know Crackle, and we also know Pop. They're the three mascots of the popular breakfast cereal, Rice Krispies.

But back in the day, there was a 4th animated character. His name was Pow.

Yes, we had Snap, Crackle, Pop, and Pow.

The first one, Snap, appeared on cereal boxes in 1941, and the others soon joined. They didn't look like they do today. In fact, instead of elves, some have described their appearance as similar to gnomes.

And all three wore little chef hats. Today only Snap sports that headwear, while Crackle goes the beanie route (cool!) and Pop has his band hat.

But wait: Who's this Pow dude?

It was the early 1950s when Kellogg's introduced a spaceman character named Pow. Apparently that era's fascination with space (this was a few years before Sputnik and the space race) spilled over into breakfast cereal. And at the time, Rice Krispies sponsored a TV show called "Space Cadet."

Pow's role was to display the "power of whole grain rice." And, side note: He never spoke a word; he only pointed at things.

Sadly, he lasted for only two commercials before blasting off into cereal mascot oblivion.

Trivia Snacks

Snap, Crackle, and Pop began a flurry of new cereal mascots. The same ad agency behind the little guys also dreamed up some other breakfast icons.

The white-mustached Cap'N Crunch showed up in 1963 and became so popular that they launched a comic book around him.

But the good Cap'N has a full name. Check his ID and you'll see that he is officially Horatio Magellan Crunch. And his ship? Why, he sails the Sea of Milk aboard the S.S. Guppy.

Cap'N Crunch was actually created by the same team that brought us Rocky and Bullwinkle, George of the Jungle, and The Mr. Peabody and Sherman Show (Google 'em, kids).

A controversy raged a few years ago when people pointed out that, according to Navy ranks, someone with three stripes on their uniform (as Crunch does) is technically a commander, not a captain.

Tony the Tiger didn't just get handed the job as spokesperson—er, spokescat. They introduced him with two other characters: Katy the Kangaroo and Elmo the Elephant. It was left up to consumers to pick their favorite, and Tony took home the prize. Katy and Elmo? Nobody knows what happened to them. Retired to the cereal farm, I suppose.

Lucky Charms came along in 1964, and naturally, they needed their hero. That's when Lucky the Leprechaun was born—although his official name is L.C. Leprechaun. He's morphed a bit through the years, but so has the cereal. They originally made it with oat pieces shaped like the stars, moons, and clovers you're used to, but also had things like arrowheads, bells, and even fish. Oh, and the marshmallow parts you know and love? In the early days those were chopped up pieces of another classic product: Circus Peanuts.

The campaign to introduce Lucky the Leprechaun spent a ton of money, making sure that he appeared not only in commercials for the cereal, but in comic books and Sunday comic strips.

Another mascot, the super-suave Sugar Bear, first showed up touting a cereal called Sugar Crisp. That was later changed to Super Sugar Crisp, and for good reason: The cereal was noted for having a whopping *51%* sugar content. Once sugar became a bad word, Post changed the name to Golden Crisp—except in Canada, where it's still Sugar Crisp.

The bear, however, continues to swagger his way through advertisements. One person observed that Sugar Bear is the Matthew McConaughey of mascots.

Trix cereal, originally known as Kix, got the memo about mascots, and in 1955 their ad agency toyed around with a puppet rabbit. Not long after that he was animated, and Tricks, the Trix Rabbit was born.

Endlessly thwarted by children when he tried to sneak off with their cereal, they mercilessly taunted him with cries of, "Silly rabbit, Trix are for kids!"

Thanks to clever marketing—including a few "Let the Rabbit eat Trix" campaigns—he occasionally got a taste.

The golden age of the mascots, however, couldn't last forever. Eventually, advocates for healthy choices zeroed in on these colorful characters. Groups lobbied to reduce advertising aimed squarely at children if it promoted unhealthy food choices. And soon the lovable mascots became less and less visible.

In 2006, several food manufacturers, including fast-food restaurants, gave in to pressure that using mascots to promote unhealthy food was unethical. They have enacted more laws that essentially put the colorful mascots out of work.

Wait . . . is the Trix Rabbit looking at me?

In 2014, a study suggested that the cereal companies were even more ingenious when it came to manipulating kids. Since most of the children's cereals were on middle shelves, they designed the boxes so the mascots were looking slightly downward.

Right into the faces of children standing in the aisles.

In comparison, characters that appealed to adults had their gaze angled slightly upward.

Why is this important? Because tons of research showed that eye contact—even with animated characters—helped to develop brand loyalty.

Time Zones

Hey, what time is it? Well, it depends on where you live, right? Today we take our various time zones for granted, but it used to be a giant mess.

In this chapter you'll learn:

- Railroads forced us to coordinate our time
- The number of time zones in the world
- How it can be the same time in Florida as it is in Oregon

So why did it used to be so difficult to keep track of the time ? Because once upon a time (ha!) cities and towns used to select *their own* time, and they usually based it on when the sun crossed the midpoint of the sky. They gave one person in town the chore of noticing when the sun was straight overhead, they'd set one big clock, and then everyone would coordinate with it.

This wasn't a problem, because there wasn't any transportation that would get you anywhere fast enough to notice a difference. If it took weeks or months to go from one part of the country to another, nobody quibbled over an hour or two.

We also had no instantaneous communication: No phones, no radio, no TV, no Internet. You had to write a letter to communicate with someone even a few miles away, so time didn't really matter.

Ah, but once the railroads began crisscrossing the world, and once telegraph lines went up, everything changed. Suddenly we needed to coordinate our time.

It's not like everything was simple in the beginning, though. Each local train station still set their own clock, so at one point there were about 300 different "times" around the United States. This obviously confused everyone who traveled, and something had to be done.

The head of the national weather service suggested four time zones across the U.S. The railroads, who needed something to coordinate their schedules, agreed.

At noon on November 18th, 1883, a telegraph operator in Chicago sent out time signals to major cities in each zone, and we officially got our time act together.

Globally, a group of scientists put their heads together to consider the problem. Since it took 24 hours for our planet to rotate 360 degrees, they broke up the world into 24 time zones, each stretching about 15 degrees in longitudinal width.

The distance is greatest at the equator, and shrinks as it approaches both of the poles. At the equator, the distance around the world is 24,902 miles, so each time zone measures about 1,038 miles.

The imaginary lines that break up each zone begin with one that runs through Greenwich, a suburb of London. Thus, you may have heard of Greenwich Mean Time, or Coordinated Universal Time.

Trivia Snacks

How many time zones are there around the world? As we've learned, technically there are 24 time zones worldwide. But some countries refuse to use the international zones created in the 1800s. China, for instance, insists on the time remaining the same across the entire country, even though it stretches through three standard zones.

Other countries break up their own time zones into smaller increments, so the time could be 30 minutes or 45 minutes different from one location to another.

Making it even more complicated is the fact that some countries acknowledge Daylight Saving Time, while others do not.

How many time zones are there in the United States? Technically, there are nine.

Confused? Well, there are the four most familiar ones in the continental U.S. (Eastern, Central, Mountain, and Pacific), but don't forget about Alaska Time and Hawaii/Aleutian Time. That makes six.

Then you have the time zones that cover some of the country's territories. There's a different time zone for Puerto Rico and the U.S. Virgin Islands, another for American Samoa, and yet another for Guam.

Hey, what do they do in Antarctica? Yes, there are American research stations near the south pole, and they tend to sync their time with the nearest supply base in New Zealand.

Who's in charge of the time? Well, in the U.S. the time zone boundaries and the overseeing of Daylight Saving Time/Standard Time is handled by the Department of Transportation.

The official timekeeping services are rendered by the National Institute of Standards and Technology (NIST) and the U.S. Naval Observatory. They keep their clocks synchronized with each other and with those of other countries.

And last, my favorite Trivia Snack regarding time in the continental United States:

Did you know that for one hour each year it's the exact same time in Florida and Oregon? Okay, just tiny parts of those two states, but still.

It's because the dividing lines for the time zones are not straight lines. They zig and they zag. And there's actually a small part of Oregon that's in the Mountain time zone, and there's a snippet of the Florida panhandle that lies in the Central time zone.

So each November, when we "fall back" from Daylight Saving Time into Standard Time at 2 a.m., those Central time zone towns in the Florida panhandle share the same hour as everyone in the Mountain zone.

Which includes that little portion of Oregon. So for 60 minutes you have an Atlantic coast state that shares time with a Pacific coast state. Cool.

Flying Spiders

It's often called ballooning, or kiting, and it's one of the most unusual forms of transportation in the world. Little spiders have been doing it since the Cretaceous period, for at least 100 million years.

In this chapter you'll learn:

- Why they take flight
- Just how far they can go
- Surprise! They're not using the wind to take off

Like millions of people around the world, I thoroughly enjoyed reading *Charlotte's Web* as a kid. The classic story by E. B. White ends with (oops, spoiler!) hundreds of Charlotte's spider babies launching themselves into the air using this technique called ballooning.

What are they doing? It's not just in fiction. For years scientists have studied these aviation marvels, wondering how and why the arachnids do it.

Newly hatched spiders will stick their rumps into the air, uncoil a length of webbing (like Spiderman) from their spinnerets, and create a little silk parachute to lift themselves skyward.

When they think they've found a suitable spot, they'll use that same silk as a drag against the air to slow themselves, and then take advantage of its stickiness to grasp a leaf or branch.

Why are they doing it? The same reasons other animals roam about: Dispersing the species and searching for a fresh spot to set up shop. When you get hundreds—or thousands—of spiderlings congregated in one area, ballooning becomes a matter of survival.

Go where there aren't hundreds of competitors wandering around, right?

In some parts of the world, it's not unusual for millions upon millions of little hatchlings to take to the skies, using balloons that stretch for as much as one meter in length. When they all land, the vast amount of spider silk left on the ground can look like a light dusting of snow.

Shocking news: They're not using the wind to launch themselves. For centuries it was thought the baby spiders were using the wind to lift off. Then it was assumed they were riding thermal lifts, the way birds will find elevators of warm air rising, and ride them up.

But no. In fact, if there's more than even a very light breeze, they won't set sail at all. They'll wait till the wind dies down.

Scientists believe it's all about electricity. The Earth has a negative charge, while the air above us holds a positive charge. When the spider climbs to the top of a branch or fence post, it unfurls a silk strand shaped almost like a fan. And that little silk fan, like the ground, sports a negative charge.

Recall your elementary school science class: Two magnets of the same charge will repulse each other. It may be that the spiders are using these electrostatic forces for launch, and then riding light breezes to their ultimate destination.

Plus, the higher they go, the more of an electrical gradient they'll encounter, an increase of as much as 100 volts per meter. It's well known that many insects are not only aware of electrical fields, but use them for their navigation and other jobs. Honey bees use electrical charges to communicate with their hive. Well, spiders use it to fly.

Trivia Snacks

There's more of them airborne than you think. A study in the 1920s found that 1 out of every 17 invertebrates flying through the air was a spider.

Better pack a lunch. While most baby spiders aren't traveling far at all—sometimes just a few meters away from their nest—others go a LONG way.

Charles Darwin famously found them landing on the HMS Beagle, 60 miles offshore. But they've also been found two-and-a-half miles up into the atmosphere, and have traveled as far as a thousand miles. Studies show the little guys can travel without food for more than three weeks.

What happens when they find themselves hundreds of miles out at sea? Many species have water-repellent legs, which allow them to ride on the tops of the waves. Once a breeze comes along, they'll raise their abdomens and use them as sails to propel them until they (hopefully) reach a nice dry spot.

The silk begins as a liquid. Sure, it shoots out of a spider like a batch of silly string, but when it's inside the spider's body, the silk is actually a liquid form of protein. And you won't believe how strong it is.

Don't be fooled by its dainty appearance; pound for pound —well, gram for gram—spider silk is up to *five times* stronger than steel. It's just that it's so thin, one strand that wrapped around the Earth's equator would only weigh a little over a pound.

Their silk is quite versatile, too. When we think of spiders and their webs, we tend to think they produce just one type of silk and use that for everything.

But no. The average spider might produce *seven* different varieties of silk, each for a different purpose. These various types each come from a separate gland. More than one is often used in building their web, depending on the specific area of need (connecting lines, support lines). They also have a different variety for wrapping their prey.

Oh, and a different type for their flying.

Antarctica

The frozen continent around the South Pole, the place we automatically associate with giant blocks of ice, has had a surprising history. Today, it operates as a place of scientific study, a true cooperative effort between several countries.

In this chapter you'll learn:

- Antarctica is actually a desert . . .
- . . . but it used to be a jungle
- It has lakes that might teach us about Jupiter

For years, the coldest place on Earth was the only continent without a name.

What to call it? Well, it wasn't formally "discovered" until the 19th century. Before that time it was only *rumored* to exist. Aristotle even mentioned "an Antarctic region" in about 350 B.C.

People in the 15th century referred to this imagined land mass as Terra Australis, which is Latin for "Southern Land." Nobody had seen it, but the theory was that something had to be down there, if only to "balance out" the land in Europe and Asia. Yes, that's often how science worked.

In the early 1800s, the governor of New South Wales in Sydney decided THEY should adopt the name Terra Australis and morph it into Australia. So they did.

That meant the hypothetical land around the southern pole lost its name, and went without one for decades. In the late 1800s, they finally dubbed it Antarctica—Greek for "Opposite to the North." Okay, not so clever, but at least it gave the place an identity.

But what's this about Antarctica being a desert? That word often conjures images of sand dunes and camels, so you'd think with all that ice—and there's a LOT of it—that it would be far from a desert.

But no. Antarctica is not only the coldest spot on Earth, but also the driest. The continent averages only about 7 to 8 inches of precipitation a year, and then only at the coast.

There are places in the interior that haven't seen rain for about two million years. *Two million*!

Does anyone "own" Antarctica? No, and that's one thing that makes it a pretty cool place. There isn't a single nation on Earth that can claim ownership of the continent.

Technically, Antarctica falls under the term "condominium," which in this case means that multiple nations agree to share the territory and exercise all the rights equally.

All of that is regulated by The Antarctic Treaty, which was originally signed in 1959 by 12 countries. Since then another 38 have joined.

The treaty became necessary when tensions escalated during the Cold War. So many scientific and military activities were going on that things could've turned nasty.

Is this where I say "cooler" heads prevailed? Sorry.

Trivia Snacks

Antarctica gets high. Besides the brutally cold conditions, it's also the windiest continent on the planet, the driest, and the highest. At least when it comes to average altitude.

The ice shelf in some places is almost three miles thick, and averages about 1.2 miles.

Did it really used to have forests? Yep. It's hard for us to imagine today, but Antarctica used to be a tropical zone.

You have to go way back, about 170 million years ago, when it was part of the supercontinent known as Gondwana. The sections we today call Antarctica hovered around the equator, and that means that plants, forests, and animals thrived.

About the time when the dinosaurs perished, 66 million years ago, Antarctica broke away from Gondwana and present-day Australia and scooted down to the South Pole to take the spot we know today.

There are lakes in Antarctica. Although there is actual land in Antarctica (including volcanic rock), we best know it for the thick layers of ice. About 90% of all the ice on Earth is situated on this one continent, along with 70% of the planet's fresh water.

Below that ice, however, there are lakes—hundreds of them. The largest, called Vostok, is (by volume) the 6th largest lake in the world.

But the surface of this lake lies almost two miles below solid ice, so the pressures are intense. In other words, you won't be going swimming there anytime soon.

However, scientists are anxiously studying these subterranean lakes because they may turn out to resemble the kinds of lakes we find on the moons of Jupiter and Saturn.

And if life can exist in Lake Vostok, who's to say it couldn't be flourishing on some far away moon?

It gets more tourists than you might think. While it may not hold a lot of charm for people who prefer sun and sand on their vacations, Antarctica *does* have an appeal for some hardy souls.

Pre-COVID, the continent received more than 40,000 tourists a year. That's up considerably from the 5,000 who visited back in 1990.

Who lives in Antarctica? At any given time there are between 1,000 and 5,000 people working on the continent. Most are researchers, scientists, and support staff, living and working at the 66 (as of the year 2020) various stations. The largest of these has a population of over 1,300 people, but other outposts may have as few as six individuals. Sheesh, you better get along well.

Besides the humans, Antarctica is home to seals, whales, some albatross, and, of course, penguins. About 12 million of the flightless birds call the ice their home.

But no polar bears. Sorry, that's the other pole.

Commercials

Often criticized, sometimes entertaining, but ever present. Seems you can't go two minutes without being assaulted with someone selling you something.

In this chapter you'll learn:

- The number of ads you see each day
- The first-ever radio and television commercials
- Why the burger in the ad looks different

You think they're a product of our times, but commercials are not a modern invention.

Would you believe the ancient Egyptians used advertising? They created sales messages on papyrus. They even made posters to peddle their goods.

In ancient China, the advertising was verbal. And in Europe, some businesses employed town criers, who normally announced important events, but could be hired to spread the messages of merchants, too.

That's not much different from the boys hired by newspapers in the early 20th century to holler out that day's headlines in order to entice people to part with their nickel.

The early 19th century saw the first advertising agencies, businesses whose sole purpose is to manage the creative attempts of companies to lure new customers. One of their earliest tactics was to buy up large chunks of advertising space in newspapers in order to get a discounted rate, then turn around and sell that space to various companies.

The advertising industry is considered one of the pioneers in bringing more women into the workforce. Why? Because agencies recognized that women were responsible for the bulk of the purchases made by their households, so their insight and input was extremely valuable.

In fact, a woman named Helen Landsdowne is credited with coming up with one of the first ads to employ sex appeal. Her ad for a soap brand titillated readers with the tag line, "Skin You Love to Touch." It was not only a hit, but was named one of the top 50 advertising campaigns of all time. From that point on, advertisers were convinced that sex sells.

It wasn't long before psychology was employed, too. Experts in the field were consulted when producing ads, and found that appealing to the customers' emotions often produced a desire to buy. To this day, psychology is an important element in crafting a winning commercial.

How can you measure an ad's effectiveness? It's challenging. Different commercials have different intentions and calls to action. Is it meant to sell a product? Is it about simply building brand recognition?

Ad agencies employ people to analyze data from before and after an ad campaign. Some of the most successful campaigns in history were never meant to be hits; they just happened to click, for whatever reason, with the public. Recreating this magic, however, has often proved elusive.

Once companies realized just how much time people spent online, staring at their screens, they pounced. Suddenly all your "free" content online was peppered with pop-up after pop-up. We've all visited sites that are, inch for inch, way more populated with ads than with actual content.

All of this inspired the creation of apps to block advertising. And the effect?

Online companies claim it costs them billions of dollars in revenue each year.

Trivia Snacks

How many commercials do we see each day? Hold on to your hat—the numbers will shock you.

Back in the 1970s, it was estimated that we were exposed to as many as 1,500 messages a day. By the early 21st century, that number was up to 5,000.

As of 2020, some industry experts believe you're confronted with 6,000 to 10,000 advertisements every day —and you're often not even aware of it.

Where are they all coming from? TV ads, radio, billboards, pop-ups on videos, social media sites, phone screens, magazines, direct mail pieces. And it goes on and on.

In fact, as a society we've become absolutely numb to the non-stop flood of sales pitches. It's just part of our everyday lives, like background noise or wallpaper. Even our clothing is covered with ads. Shoe brands, shirt brands, labels on purses, logos on hats, bumper stickers on cars.

What was the first radio ad? Accounts differ, but it's generally accepted that the first official radio ad was an attempt to sell real estate, specifically some apartments in the New York area. It aired on WEAF in 1922.

The first television ad? It was July 1941, just before the start of a baseball game televised between the Brooklyn Dodgers and Philadelphia Phillies. For $9, the Bulova company ran a 10-second ad for their watches.

Why does food look different in TV ads? Yes, you may have noticed that your fast-food burger doesn't look like the one in the ad. It can't. It literally can't. Because the one in the commercial often isn't even edible. It's made with props, and sometimes pinned together—yes, actual pins—to make it stand up taller and firmer.

Fizzy substances (like antacids) can be added to make sodas look, well, fizzier. Ice cream commercials sometimes use modeling clay or mashed potatoes, because those won't melt during the long days of filming.

And when all is said and done, the post-production process goes to work to dress up the product even more.

Gimme more. Given all of this, there is one statistic that stands out. In a survey, 9% of people claimed there were *not enough* commercials on the radio. They preferred more.

Electric Cars

It may be hard to believe, but electric cars are not a new idea. In fact, they were around before the Model T. And, since the average person drives less than 50 miles a day, overnight charging will be plenty for as much as 90% or 95% of households.

In this chapter you'll learn:

- Electric cars were a hit before gas-powered cars
- Their eerily quiet days may be at an end
- The first ET car was an EV

Electric car sales are growing, although they have a ways to go before they catch up with traditional gasoline engines. As of 2019, the total market share of electric vehicles (EV) in the United States was a little over 2%.

But did you know that at one point their share was *33%*?

Yep, a *third* of vehicles on the road were quiet little electric cars.

The year was 1900. Folks like Thomas Edison were big believers in EV. Henry Ford even looked into it. For a while, the future for battery-driven cars looked rosy.

Then it came crashing down. Why? For one thing, Ford unveiled the Model T, which was only a third of the price of an EV.

Plus, all that Texas crude oil was cheap. It became easier and more affordable for people to drive long distances with gas engines. The electric dream died for almost 70 years.

Makes you wonder where we'd be today if we'd spent the last century developing the technology.

More and more countries are setting timetables to ban the sale of gasoline-powered automobiles. Many are looking at having laws in place between 2035 and 2050, but others are more aggressive. Norway, for instance, has declared that 2025 is the last year you'll be able to purchase a car powered by fossil fuels. As of 2020, electric cars already made up more than half of car sales each month in Norway.

For many people, one attraction of electric vehicles is how quiet they are. However, that also poses a potentially dangerous element for cyclists and pedestrians. If you've ever looked behind you in a parking lot and been surprised to see that an electric car snuck up behind you, you know what I'm talking about.

Well, those days are coming to an end. New laws require manufacturers to add some sort of artificial noise as a warning to pedestrians, sounds that kick in when the car is going slower than 19 miles per hour. The sound would only be heard on the outside—so your cockpit will remain mostly silent. But isn't it funny that after a century of striving to make cars quieter, we now have to artificially make them noisier?

What drives up the cost of electric cars is the battery pack. Ah, but those days are rapidly ending as the price of batteries plummets. Just a few years ago a standard EV battery might cost as much as $30,000. Today, it's falling below $10,000, making electric cars much more competitive with combustion engine vehicles. One EV might have as much as 30% of its cost tied up with the battery only. Some say the price drop is the tipping point that will drive huge sales.

Trivia Snacks

One of the earliest pioneers of electric cars was Ferdinand Porsche. Perhaps you've heard of his sports cars? He thought electric cars were a great idea, and he introduced the P1 in 1898.

Porsche also created the first hybrid, a combo gas-electric system. These people were WAY ahead of their time.

It took the oil embargo/gas shortage of 1973 to shock governments into action. Until then, gas was cheap and plentiful. But suddenly lines at gas stations stretched for miles, people were panicked, and governments around the world said *Uh oh, we have a problem.*

In the U.S., Congress passed an act in 1976 to support research into hybrid and electric cars. Today, several automakers are investing billions to return us to the dream of the late 1800s.

Where will you "fill up"? Of course, if you're going to drive an electric car, you need charging stations. As of 2020, there were 26,000 of these around the United States, consisting of about 84,000 outlets. Worldwide, the number of plugs surpassed the one million mark in 2020. And, not surprisingly, many traditional gas stations have added—or are adding—EV charging ports.

Some countries are charging ahead (sorry, had to) when it comes to EV. The Netherlands, for example, has more charging stations than the U.S., despite having a population smaller than the state of New York.

Yet 95% of EV charging takes place at home, so the market for installing fast-charge systems in garages is growing.

Charging while driving? Yep. There are plans in place to create charging pads beneath certain roads and highways, and in places like fast-food drive-thru lanes. Just like you'd put a phone on a charging pad, your car could get the same treatment just by driving down the road.

The first extra-terrestrial car was an EV. Astronauts on the Apollo 15 mission in 1971 had the honor, and the next two missions followed suit.

They drove a battery-powered Lunar Roving Vehicle (LRV), what would soon become known as the *Moon Buggie*.

The LRVs were built by the Boeing company (yeah, the airplane folks), and reached a top speed on the lunar surface of about 11 mph.

Those three electric cars are still parked there on the moon, just waiting for drivers to return.

Buttons and Holes

Not gonna lie: When I told my wife that I was putting together a chapter on buttons and buttonholes, she was underwhelmed. But then I shared some of the fun facts, and she perked right up. I think you will, too.

In this chapter you'll learn:

- We got buttons long before the holes
- Why men and women have them on opposite sides
- Snotty noses inspired some uses

Might as well get the most humorous fun fact out of the way first, and the one that surprises people the most:

Buttons have been around for thousands of years—but button*holes* didn't show up until 800 years ago. That's just funny to me, but once you explore the history, it makes sense.

It all starts with understanding that our first use of buttons had nothing to do with fastening clothes. No, anthropologists think buttons may have begun purely as *decoration*. So people in this era looked remarkably sparkly and stylish, although their pants may have constantly fallen down around their ankles.

And, once someone had the bright idea to use them to fasten shirts, pants, and coats, they didn't use holes; they used loops. Button*holes*, the actual slits sewn into fabric, were used to a small extent by early Romans to connect some of their leatherwork. But buttonholes didn't become standard practice until some folks in Germany got the bright idea.

Who had the idea for buttons first? The archaeological record says buttons first showed up during the Bronze Age in southern Asia, near what today is Pakistan. Not long after, they spread to China and areas of Scotland.

By 4,000 years ago, buttons were being made from seashells—and that's still a common material used today. The Egyptians even crafted them from metals.

Buttons were also made from wood, ivory, gold, glass, and even bone. But they were still mostly ornamental, even sewn into wigs.

In the 19th century, people considered button making an art form. In fact, to this day you can find historical button displays at the Victoria and Albert Museum, as well as the Smithsonian.

And in 1852, celebrated author Charles Dickens set aside his novel in progress to write an article on the button industry in Birmingham, England.

Trivia Snacks

Why are buttons on one side for men, and on the other side for women? First of all, it's funny that so many people don't know this is even a thing. Try asking a friend and see if they know.

Buttons for men's clothes are generally on the right (when you're wearing them), and for women they're on the left.

Why? Could the answer really be swords and babies? Some theories (because nobody knows for sure) claim that men needed to be able to draw their sword with their right hand, so they'd have to use their left to quickly unbutton their tunics.

Women, because their dominant hand was usually the right, would hold a child on their left side, and therefore needed their right hand to open their tops. Makes sense, right?

Another theory holds that it was more a product of wealthy women being dressed by servants. Since the servants were generally right hand dominant, it was easier for them to dress their ladies if the buttons were on her left side.

Whatever the reason, the results haven't changed in centuries, and now it's just the way it is.

What about buttons on sleeves? Stories contradict who was responsible for those brass buttons on the sleeves of military coats—was it Napoleon, or Prussia's Frederick the Great? Regardless, the explanation is that some great military leader was tired of his officers wiping their mouths or their snotty noses on the sleeves of their uniforms.

So they ordered brass buttons to be sewn into the sleeves, assuring that anyone who tried to wipe mucus or leftover lunch onto them would feel the pain.

I'm sorry, but whether that's true or not, I WANT it to be true.

For what it's worth, legend has it that Napoleon also invented French Cuffs. These allowed his soldiers to wipe their noses, then fold the sleeves back onto themselves in the style of a cuff.

Were Napoleon's soldiers always sick or something?

Other clever uses? Speaking of wars, soldiers in both WWI and WWII used buttons as lockets. Inside these, they kept tiny compasses.

One of the most ingenious uses for buttons began in the 17th century. Box-like buttons were built into clothing and used to smuggle illegal substances, including drugs, across borders.

It won't surprise you at all to learn that the practice is actually still attempted today. Just ask your friendly customs official. They've seen it all.

And, of course, we must acknowledge that there are other types of buttons. These are the ones we pin on our shirts and coats to proudly proclaim how much *We Like Ike*, or to support the home team, or to simply say something funny.

But the most valuable buttons of this type go all the way back to the 18th century. At an auction in Dallas in 2018, a set of buttons created to celebrate the 1789 inauguration of George Washington as President of the United States sold for about a quarter of a million dollars.

The buttons helped set a world record for the highest grossing auction of political memorabilia.

Money

It's been the subject of songs, plays, and movies, and while some say it's the root of all evil, people sure seem to want to get their hands on as much of it as they can.

In this chapter you'll learn:

- How long dollar bills last
- Whose face is on the most forms of currency
- Apparently rats love the stuff

For ages the standard form of money was the coin, stamped out of precious metals like gold or silver. But eventually merchants and banks got tired of hauling around big, heavy bags.

A different form of currency took hold, what we today call paper money.

The first to offer this form of currency, originally known as a promissory note, may have been the Carthaginians around the 2nd century BC. China produced their promissory notes on leather, as did the Romans.

The Romans, by the way, also paid their soldiers in salt, which was quite valuable at the time. Since the Latin word for salt was *sal*, they were issued a monthly stipend called a *salarium*. From this, we got the word *salary*.

The first known version of an actual banknote showed up in China in the 7th century. It took another 400 years for currency to actually be printed on paper, though. Then European travelers, like Marco Polo, are believed to have brought the idea to the West.

Sadly, paper money invited forgers. And they were only too happy to try their hand at copying the real thing.

Of course, back in the day even coins were in danger of being faked. Ingenious criminals would melt them down, then mix just a little of the precious metal into a mold with a more base (cheaper) metal and pass these off as the real thing. They'd then sell the rest of the good stuff for a profit.

But with paper, you needed only a talented artist. And, once the copy machine came on the scene, there was a rush to see who could pump out giant stacks of phony money.

Sometimes it takes a village. In 2016, the Treasury Department reported that a counterfeiting ring in Peru had been busted. Nearly 50 people were arrested and 1,600 printing plates were confiscated.

And how much cash? They had around $30 million in U.S. phony money, and 50,000 Euros.

A former counterfeiter claims teams like this can have as many as ten experts working on a single project, from designers to artists to printers to cutters.

Trivia Snacks

How much money is in circulation? As of 2019, close to $2 *trillion* United States dollars were floating around the world. The bulk of that is overseas. If you count the cash from *all* countries, it's around $5 trillion.

And, when you factor in things like bank accounts, savings accounts, and other forms of "broad money," it's more like $80 trillion.

How long does a U.S. bill last before it's recycled? It fluctuates, and it depends on the denomination. But a $1 bill generally lasts around 4 to 6 years.

For a C-Note, it's more like 15 to 20 years.

Coins can survive much longer. When they get recycled, they're melted down and re-cast into new coins, while the paper money is simply destroyed.

How much is actually made each year? For U.S. dollars, in 2020 the mint cranked out about 1.5 *billion* one-dollar bills, while the $20 bill had the most, with about 1.7 billion.

The bill that gets the least amount of love? That would be the $50 bill; they made "only" about 236 million of those in 2020.

Word has it that the Parker Brothers company prints more Monopoly money each year than the U.S. government prints the real thing. And you know what? It's true. Each year the game company spits out about $30 billion in multi-colored bills.

How many currencies are there? As of 2018, the United Nations recognized 180 different currencies being used in 195 countries.

What about the faces on money? Congress passed a law in 1866 that no living person could appear on American currency. This was actually a reaction to an official of the U.S. Treasury at the time who snuck his own photo onto a five-cent bill.

Whose face appears on the most currency around the world? That honor belongs to Queen Elizabeth II. Her image has graced the coinage of at least 35 different countries, ranging from Canada to Hong Kong to the Cayman Islands.

The most counterfeited bill? If you're talking outside the U.S., it's the American $100.

Within the United States, the most-counterfeited currency is the $20.

Getting caught making phony money can mean a sentence of anywhere from a few years to *life* in prison. Some countries aren't messing around.

Oh, rats! Infamous drug cartel leader Pablo Escobar is reported to have had so much cash hidden in warehouses and in fields that each year he lost more than a *billion* dollars—simply because rats ate it.

Mushrooms

Whether you call them fungi, toadstools, or the common mushroom, people around the world really like them.

In this chapter you'll learn:

- They're the oldest life forms on land
- One of them is the largest life form on Earth
- They keep us from being buried by the dead

Scientists are pretty sure that fungus were the first life forms to leave the water and establish a foothold on dry land, more than a billion years ago. Plants didn't follow for another 500 million years, and when they did, the fungus developed a productive relationship with them.

Together, they altered not only the surface of the planet, but manipulated the makeup of the atmosphere, raising the amount of oxygen and lowering the carbon dioxide, which paved the way for animals like us.

Yes, we basically owe our existence to the prep work done by mushrooms and plants.

And how do we show our gratitude? We eat them. Either on the plate at a five-star restaurant, or topping a cheesy, greasy 14-inch pizza, they are a culinary hit.

They're really big business, too. Especially for one particular county in the United States.

If you love to eat the tasty treats, you can thank the state of Pennsylvania, which produces about two-thirds of the mushrooms grown in the U.S.

And Chester County is responsible for a huge chunk of that.

Mushrooms make up the largest agricultural crop in the state—more than half-a-billion dollars every year (as of 2019).

Why does this one little corner of the world pump out so many of them? Probably because of the blood connection. Most of the mushroom businesses here are family-owned, with several generations of kids who were raised harvesting the fungi, passing along their skills right down the line.

And here's the kicker: It's not an easy crop to grow.

Today, technology has stepped in to meet the enormous worldwide demand. Computers monitor each point in the process, assuring the best output and the yummiest quality.

Did you know that the part you see—the fruiting part of the mushroom—is just the tip of the iceberg? The rest of the organism, the mycelium, can often be part of a massive underground network.

Trivia Snacks

It was a florist who started the whole thing. His name was William Swayne, a florist who first got the idea to grow mushrooms under the benches in his greenhouse. The year was 1885.

How many kinds are there? There may be as many as 50,000 different species of mushrooms around the world. Many of them are molds or yeast.

The largest living organism on our planet is a mushroom. Not a redwood tree, not a blue whale. A mushroom. Take a trip to the Blue Mountains of Oregon in the U.S. and you'll find a specific honey fungus. Underground, it spreads for nearly two-and-a-half miles (nearly four kilometers). The honey fungus is an invasive species, and it's known to kill trees and other plants while it's colonizing.

The flip side, however, is that chefs find the fruiting part of it delicious.

How many are poisonous? Well, about 20% will make you sick. And about 1% to 2% can be deadly. (So don't take one you find on the hiking trail and pop it in your mouth.)

Yes, some feature hallucinogenic qualities, ya big hippie. But it's the medicinal purposes that excite many people in the medical field. The Lion's Mane variety, for instance, has shown promise in helping people with nerve damage.

They keep us from living amongst the dead. Fungi have existed for about a billion years. To put that in perspective, trees haven't been around for even half as many years. And in all those years, fungi have helped to decompose the various plants and animals that die and fall to the ground.

Without their decomposing abilities, all of those plant and animal corpses would be stacked pretty high by now. Plus, by breaking down the dead, fungi deliver an important component to the life cycle across the planet.

Did you know mushrooms are often parasites? It's not unusual to spot them growing out of trees, both alive and dead—although they're known to sometimes kill their hosts, too.

Then there are some of the more grisly species, like the *Cordyseps sinensis*, which will sprout out of a caterpillar's body. It's like something out of a horror movie, developing inside insect larvae before popping out like a certain movie about a deadly alien. You know which one.

Are truffles mushrooms? The short answer is no—but they are cousins. Both are in the fungi family, but truffles are tubers, the fruiting body of a subterranean ascomycete fungus. Got it? Plus, what they really are is expensive, sometimes going for more than $1,000 per pound. Why?

Because they're (a) hard to find, (b) difficult to grow, and (c) a pain in the butt to store.

And I saved the best for last: **Mushrooms are closer to humans on the tree of life than they are to plants.** It's true. Fungi and animals share a common ancestor, and split away from plants on the evolutionary tree about a billion years ago. So you have more in common with a mushroom than the mushroom does with a plant.

Mirrors

The joy of narcissists, the bearer of bad luck, and the stealer of souls. These are all phrases that have been used to describe mirrors.

In this chapter you'll learn:

- How many animals recognize themselves in a mirror
- How much time we spend staring into them
- There are mirrors on the moon

The earliest mirrors used by humans were simply pools of water. They've even been called *reflecting pools*. In Greek mythology, Narcissus rejected romantic advances from others and instead fell in love with his own image reflected in a pool. Now you know where we get the term *narcissist*.

How do we know that's *us* when we peer into a mirror? It's a fair question. We take it for granted that we recognize ourselves in a mirror. But when we're infants, that's not the case. We have to *grow into* that awareness, usually by around the age of 18 months. Until then, we think it's another baby.

And as far as we know, there aren't many species that *can* recognize themselves in a reflection. A psychologist in 1970 devised *The Mirror Test*. Although his results have been debated for 50 years, he claims that only three species exhibit visual self-recognition: chimpanzees, orangutans, and human beings. Other scientists believe we can add dolphins and elephants to the list.

It would be so much easier if they could just tell us!

You use them probably every day, but do you know how mirrors work? Light rays obey the law of reflection, which means they'll bounce off an object and the outgoing angle of reflection will match the angle at which they arrived.

That's how we use mirrors to look around corners, or how moonlight is reflected off a pond. If it's bouncing off a smooth surface, the image remains tight and recognizable. If it's a rough surface, the light rays are diffused.

Think about the pond. When the water is still and flat, you get a good reflection. When there are choppy waves, the image is scattered and unrecognizable. That's why we want our mirrors to be hard, flat surfaces, and it's why glass works so well.

What's with the legend of broken mirrors and bad luck? For thousands of years, some people have believed that your reflection is a representation of your soul. By damaging a mirror, you're damaging your soul.

And, since ancient beliefs held that it takes seven years to regenerate a soul, you've doomed yourself to seven years of ill fortune.

This is also one of the many explanations for why vampires supposedly show no reflection in a mirror: Legend has it they have no soul to begin with.

Trivia Snacks

What are mirrors made from? As mentioned, light reflection requires a hard, smooth surface. The earliest known examples of human-made mirrors, from around 6,000 years ago, involved polished obsidian, which is essentially volcanic glass, forged in the extreme heat of lava.

Around 4,000 years ago, we began polishing copper, and that eventually led to other substances, such as bronze, silver, and even gold.

Today, they make most mirrors with glass that's coated with either silver or aluminum, which are highly reflective materials. Silver will reflect about 95% of light, while aluminum manages a solid 90%.

How much time do we spend looking in mirrors? The survey numbers are all over the place, but it appears (sorry) that it's around five hours per week.

In some countries it's considerably more. One survey found that Italian men invest as much as six or seven hours a week gazing into them.

You probably don't know how many mirrors you encounter on a daily basis. Sure, your bathroom, other places in your house, etc. But there's also your car's rearview mirror, the vanity mirrors in the car's sun visor, the side mirrors.

Then there are mirrors at work, in public restrooms, and at the gym. Don't forget all the mirrors arranged purely for decoration.

How do two-way mirrors work? They've always been popular in police movies and TV shows, where the suspect is interrogated while others watch in the next room.

Two-way mirrors are constructed in pretty much the same way as a traditional mirror, but the amount of silver backing is reduced. This allows most of the light to be reflected, as in a regular mirror, while a portion of it seeps through.

In most cases, they keep the person being interviewed in a bright room, while the observers next door are in a mostly darkened room. This amplifies the effect.

It's the same principal you'll notice when the lights are on in your living room at night. People outside can easily see you, while it's nearly impossible for you to observe anyone outside in the dark.

There are mirrors on the moon. The Apollo astronauts left them in the early 1970s, and they're still in use today. The mirrors were set up to reflect light from laser beams installed at Earth telescopes. The laser shoots a beam of light to the moon, where it's reflected by the Apollo mirrors. By calculating the time it takes to make the round trip, scientists can tell how far away the moon is. And these measurements are precise, telling us the distance to within 1.2 inches.

Not only that, but the calculations have taught us that the moon is drifting away from us. One year after you read this sentence, the moon will have moved away by about an inch and a half.

Toothbrushes

We take them for granted today, and they're in almost every home in the world. But the design we're familiar with today had a much more humble beginning. In fact, it was basically a stick.

In this chapter you'll learn:

- A prisoner came up with the modern version
- Sales of toothbrushes were aided by war
- How many people share a toothbrush

Who first came up with the idea of brushing teeth? Whoever she or he was, we think they had the brilliant idea around 5,000 to 6,000 years ago.

In Babylonia and ancient Egypt, they used twigs. If they found one with a nice frayed end on it, even better. Then they'd simply scrape the gunk off their teeth, rinse out their mouth, and get on with their day.

Brushing with a hog? Well, technically you'd brush with the hog's hair, probably from its back. About a thousand years ago, the Chinese came up with the idea of using bristles to effectively clean teeth, and they chose hog hair to get the job done. People found little reason to switch for the next several centuries.

Occasionally, in a pinch, they'd employ horse hairs.

Westerners can thank a prisoner for the modern toothbrush. His name was William Addis, and in the late 1700s he'd been tossed in jail for inciting a riot. While languishing in his cell, he looked at a nearby broom and had a big idea.

At the time, people in England cleaned their teeth by rubbing them with a rag dipped in either water or soot. But ol' Bill thought brooms provided a better solution.

So he kept a bone from one of his prison meals and convinced a guard to bring him some bristles. After drilling holes into the bone, he wound the bristles through, then sealed them with glue. And *voila*! A modern toothbrush.

When Addis got out of jail, he began a company mass-producing toothbrushes, which stayed in his family until 1996, selling 70 million toothbrushes a year.

If it wasn't for soldiers, our teeth might be terrible. In the U.S., the introduction of nylon bristles in the 1930s should've made the sales of brushes explode.

But even though the product was better, it took the return of millions of American soldiers from WWII to improve dental hygiene. The servicemen had been drilled (sorry) on proper dental care, and their brushing routines were strictly enforced through military discipline.

Once they re-integrated with society, we all began brushing more often and with more gusto.

Trivia Snacks

Should you floss first or brush first? People may argue over this, but according to the American Dental Association (ADA), it makes no difference which you do first. As long as you do them both.

Is there a recommended duration for the brushing? Dental smartypants say twice a day, for two minutes each time. The average person, however, spends only about 45 to 60 seconds. Gotta step up that hygiene game.

Add it all up, though, and you'll spend about 924 hours of your life brushing your teeth.

How often should you change your toothbrush? Dental experts recommend a new one every three months. That makes the toothbrush industry a nearly $5 billion market worldwide.

So how many toothbrushes are thrown away every year? About 3.5 billion toothbrushes are sold each year, which means roughly the same number of the plastic dental tools end up in landfills annually.

Why aren't they recycled? Because although the plastic part may be recyclable, the bristle portion isn't. So the whole thing gets tossed.

Is it a good workout? Well, that may be stretching it a bit. But brushing three times a day for two minutes each time will burn about 3,500 calories a year.

It's electric! An inventor named Tomlinson Moseley unveiled the earliest electric toothbrush in the 1930s. He assigned the rights to a company called Motodent.

Then, in the 1950s, a Swiss company introduced what became known as the Broxodent. This contraption actually plugged into a wall socket and used live voltage. Needless to say, it wasn't a big hit, maybe because people were a little weirded out about plugging something into a socket and then sticking it in their mouth.

In 1961, however, General Electric introduced the cordless and rechargeable toothbrush, which became a hit.

Should you cover your toothbrush? For years, companies sold little helmets that would go over the head of a toothbrush, under the assumption that it kept nasty bacteria away.

It had the opposite effect. Toothbrushes need to air out in order to discourage the growth of bacteria. Covering them keeps the bristles moist, which only makes for a thriving colony of nasty bugs.

What about sharing a toothbrush? You're either someone who would share a toothbrush with another person, or it completely grosses you out. About one-fourth of people say they'd be willing to do it. Men are more open to it than women, and the younger you are, the more likely you are to consider it.

Is sharing a toothbrush bad for you? Well, it could be, although some dental specialists say if you're kissing someone you're probably exchanging plenty of bacteria, anyway.

Trees and Rings

Some are small, some are majestic. But trees have been around for 370 million years, with their earliest ancestors—mostly ferns—stretching back even further. Their remains contributed to the vast collections of coal found around the planet.

So they've been around a long time—but what's the story with their rings?

In this chapter you'll learn:

- Tree rings can tell us age and historical climate conditions
- How long trees can live
- The number of trees on the planet

They're often called growth rings, because their purpose is to provide new wood to the tree. They also act as a vascular system. Just like humans have a circulatory system to move blood, oxygen, and nutrients around the body, trees use their system in a similar way.

They need to get water, minerals, nutrients, and other organic compounds up from the soil to the highest branches and leaves. So each growing season a tree will begin building its new growth ring.

Where is this ring? That's a fair question. In case you're wondering, it's not in the center of the tree. In other words, it doesn't form in the center of the circle and push the rest outward.

Instead, the new growth ring develops on the outer edge, just inside the bark. This growth ring starts out as a lighter color, then becomes darker toward the end of the growing season. That makes it easier to count the rings.

And they tell us the tree's age? They sure can. Although some trees can have more than one growth spurt per year, we generally find one ring for each new year.

Using the growth rings of trees to determine dates and ages is known as dendrochronology. (The Greek word dendron means tree.)

In one of the most remarkable cases ever of dendrochronology, a Stradivarius violin, valued at around $20 million, had its authenticity verified—along with the origin of the wood used to craft it—through the examination of rings within the instrument.

But the rings can tell us a lot more than just their age. For one thing, they can help us chart climate history.

If an area goes through a drought, it can affect the size of the tree rings. Likewise, if the climate becomes exceptionally hot or cold for several years, we see the results in the rings.

By examining the size and shapes of a series of rings, we can determine how the climate behaved during those years.

That's how we know certain decades in the past were either much warmer, or experienced what scientists call mini-ice ages. If you see a growth ring that's fairly wide, it probably means the tree experienced a nice growing season with plenty of sunshine and abundant rain.

Who figured this out? The ancient Greeks had a pretty good idea about it. But it was Leonardo da Vinci (that dude was really smart) who first suggested that the width of tree rings was an indicator of climate conditions.

On top of that, we can also determine if a tree survived a fire. A tree will attempt to patch itself after fire damage, and that can be found in the tree rings. The same can be said for significant insect damage. It's all captured in the rings.

How can we learn a tree's age without cutting it down? Sadly, some really old trees were cut down (see a very heartbreaking story below) before scientists unveiled a technique called coring.

To core a tree, you bore a screw into the trunk. The tip of this borer is hollow, so as it's twisted inside it captures a pencil-sized section all the way to the center. Then it's twisted back out, bringing the core with it. It's very similar to ice cores that scientists take out of glaciers.

Once the core is removed, you seal the hole to prevent disease.

To keep track of worldwide climate data, there's actually an International Tree Ring Database, which compiles information on tree ring width from forests around the world.

Comparing these samples allows scientists to create accurate maps of droughts and temperature fluctuations going back up to 2,000 years.

Trivia Snacks

How long can trees live? The simple answer is thousands of years. There are many trees around the world that are well over three thousand years old.

And the oldest one we know about? The oldest known individual living tree is in the White Mountains of California. Nicknamed *Methuselah*, it's estimated to be over 4,800 years old. That makes it older than the Great Pyramid in Egypt.

But if you want a sad story: There was a bristlecone pine tree in eastern Nevada named *Prometheus*. Back in 1964, a graduate student and a member of the Forest Service cut down *Prometheus*. (The stories regarding how and why are debated.)

But once they examined the remains, they discovered that *Prometheus* had been the oldest known tree on the planet. Perhaps almost 5,000 years old.

How many trees are on Earth? Lots of numbers are thrown around, but more than one scientific journal has said it's mind boggling: The planet has approximately three TRILLION trees, or about 400 for every person on Earth.

As of this writing, worldwide we still cut down 10 billion more trees each year than we plant. But the good news is that more and more countries are taking notice and trying to turn those numbers around.

Bad Drivers

It's a known fact that *you're* the only good driver out of millions of people on the road. Am I right? So what makes a bad driver? A simple enough question, but ultimately it depends who you ask.

In this chapter you'll learn:

- Would you fail a driving test today?
- How many people are caught speeding
- Who got the first speeding ticket

Speeding is what most people immediately associate with bad drivers. More than 60% of people say you're a lousy driver if you're speeding . . and yet 40% claim they *love* to drive fast.

You should know that one in three people on the road at this very moment is convinced that speed limits are merely "a suggestion." Those are their words, by the way.

Does your driving style define your personality? Over three-quarters of people believe it's true. Nearly half say that someone who follows all the driving laws is likely a trustworthy person in general.

Sometimes it has nothing to do with the way you actually

drive. Just the way you treat your car makes an impression. Keep it clean and in good condition, and the average person will consider you to be responsible and reliable.

Would you date a bad driver? Don't laugh; more than half of people surveyed said poor driving skills are a deal-breaker in a relationship.

Trivia Snacks

Could you pass a driving test today? Your knee-jerk response might be a hearty, "Of course!" But don't be too sure. A study of 500 people discovered that more than 44% couldn't pass the written portion of the test. Women did better than men, and it wasn't that close.

By the way: Those 44% are sharing the road with you. Buckle up.

Music makes you dangerous. We love our tunes, and there's something about being in a car that makes us turn it up. But studies show that thousands of traffic accidents every year are a direct result of people fumbling with their music, either the radio or one of their devices.

But worst of all? *Singing* to the music. The theory is that singing requires your brain to concentrate on the lyrics, even if you know them by heart. Even that little bit of focus takes away enough brain power that you don't react as quickly to trouble. Sorry; you'll have to leave your singing back in the shower.

Routines are almost as dangerous. If you take the same route to work or school every day, your brain eases up and leaves you susceptible to accidents. Take an alternate route and your brain suddenly is paying much more attention. A simple change of routine can be enough to lower your chances of an accident.

How many people are speeding? I can't tell you that, but I can tell you how many get ticketed.

In an average day in the U.S., a little over 110,000 people are written up for excessive speed. That works out to almost 41 million every year.

To put *that* in perspective, speeding tickets are issued at a rate of more than one every second.

The top five reasons for getting pulled over? Number one, naturally, is speeding. Number two is an equipment violation (tint is too dark, headlight or brake light is out). Those are followed by improper lane changes, tailgating, and cell phone use.

What will get you *out* of a ticket? (Besides begging and praying—neither of which appears to work too well.) An insurance company surveyed its customers and found that the best way to talk yourself out of a moving violation is to say you didn't see the sign. Hmm. That's followed by "I'm lost and unfamiliar with this area." And yes, in the top ten is the classic "I had to go to the bathroom." Good luck.

The first recorded speeding ticket? It happened in 1899 in Manhattan, where a cab driver was flying through an eight-mile-per-hour zone at a scorching 12 mph. Dude, where's the fire?

The record for most failed driving tests? It's held by a woman in South Korea who failed 960 times before finally getting the green light. And taking the test there isn't free; she figured it cost her more than $10,000 to finally pass.

What are the top reasons for failing a driving test? Almost 20% fall into one of two categories: Either they disobeyed traffic signs, or they ran a red light. An unnecessary stop at a Yield sign can also do it.

The other biggie is going too fast or too slow. The folks giving the test say the slowpokes are usually nervous and overly cautious. Because of this, some states now post *minimum* speed limits on highways.

How much do driving instructors make? As with many things, it depends where you are. But as of 2020, the U.S. national average hovered in the $18-$20 per hour range.

In some parts of the country, an instructor pulls in about $43,000 per year.

Minus, of course, the cost of antacids and hair dye to cover the gray.

Witness Protection Program

Developed to protect people from vengeful gangsters in the 1960s, today it has one of the most remarkable records in all of law enforcement.

There have been movies made about it, and the label itself is part of pop culture; but very few people understand how it actually works . . . which is intentional.

In this chapter you'll learn:

- The program is basically perfect
- How they make people disappear
- The success rate in getting convictions

In sports, we're fascinated with the idea of going undefeated. As of 2020, only two NFL teams in the modern era have managed to win every game in the regular season, and only one of those two stayed unbeaten in the postseason.

If a baseball team wins 20 games in a row, they're in very rare air. Only seven teams have done it, and only *two* since FDR was president.

All of those teams are nothing compared to the Witness Protection Program. In the fifty years it's been around, it's gone 8,600 - 0.

This federal program is administered by the United States Department of Justice and operated by the U.S. Marshals Service. The program provides protection for federal witnesses in cases involving organized crime, drug trafficking, terrorism, and other crimes.

It not only protects those witnesses, but close family members, too. In exchange for their testimony, the witness is given a new identity with new papers, and relocated to live out their life in another community somewhere within the country.

The WPP, also known as the Witness Security Program, was originally designed to be part of the Organized Crime Control Act of 1970. And there are certain stipulations. For one, the protection can only be provided for witnesses whose testimony is deemed critical (and credible) to the case, and if their life is legitimately in danger because of that testimony.

The office overseeing the program also must make another important determination: What kind of risk will the witness pose on their new community? The witness then goes through an interview process with the U.S. Marshals, and if they give the green light, it then moves on to the Attorney General, who must sign off on it.

Trivia Snacks

How are they protected during the trial itself? The Marshals can go to great lengths to protect a federal witness while shuttling them back and forth to the trial. They've been known to use helicopters, or more low-key options like mail trucks and even fishing boats. Sometimes high-profile decoys are used in front of the courthouse while the witness slips in through a back door.

How do they make a person disappear? Well, it's a big country with thousands of towns. The witness can have their pick of a new name, but they're often encouraged to use the same first name. That name change goes through the court system, just like it would for you and me, but in this case the records are sealed, preventing bad people from tracking down the witness.

How do they get a job? The Marshals will provide one "reasonable" job opportunity for the witness. But they also provide help in finding housing, and they give the witness up to $60,000 (as of 2020) in "subsistence payments."

But if the witness isn't vigilant about trying to find a job, the money is cut off and the witness will have to apply for aid like anyone else. In other words, it behooves them to shut off the television and find work.

It's not just the witness, either. Everyone in their immediate family is given new identity papers, and they're even offered therapy sessions for help in coping with the change. Medical care is covered by the government, too.

Does the program get convictions? It does, and at an impressive clip. Over the years, the Justice Department has an 89% conviction rate in cases that rely on the testimony of these witnesses. Over 10,000 hardcore criminals have been sentenced.

What if the person being protected is a criminal, too? Actually, they almost always are. In fact, the man who created the program estimated that about 95% of people in the Witness Protection Program are criminals themselves.

In that case, they inform local law enforcement in their new town of their arrival. And if these protected witnesses are already prison inmates themselves, the Federal Bureau of Prisons provides their protection.

For those who are relocated to new towns, 17% of them will break the law again (known as recidivism), which is actually much lower than the rate for paroled inmates, which is about 40%.

If convicted of the new crime and incarcerated, protection of the witness is turned over to the Bureau of Prisons. So they're still hiding—they're now just hiding in prison.

What's the success rate when it comes to protection? It's impressive beyond words. The Marshals are undefeated. In the half-century since it began, the WPP has overseen more than 8,600 people *without a single instance* of anyone being found or harmed.

And, finally, it doesn't have to be permanent. Anyone in the program may leave the protection and return to their former identity anytime they like.

But the Marshals strongly discourage this.

I hope you've enjoyed this! It's easy to get more Fun Facts and Trivia Snacks.

Turn the page to find out how.

BBG

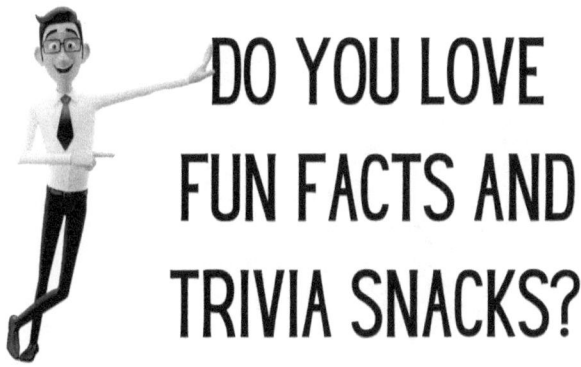

DO YOU LOVE FUN FACTS AND TRIVIA SNACKS?

Most email sucks. This does not.

Subscribe to Billy B. Good. It takes about 27 seconds.
Then you'll finally get the good stuff in your inbox.
And, you'll get a free ebook, too!

Sign up at
BillyBGood.com

More from Billy B. Good

Hope you had fun with the Fun Facts and Trivia Snacks! Are you ready for more?

I've got multiple volumes for you to enjoy, and even some special editions. Find a cornucopia of good stuff right here, including:

Billy B. Good's Fun Facts and Trivia Snacks, Volume 2

Billy B. Good's Fun Facts and Trivia Snacks, Volume 3

and

Billy B. Good's CHRISTMAS Fun Facts and Trivia Snacks

Billy B. Good's HALLOWEEN Fun Facts and Trivia Snacks

www.ingramcontent.com/pod-product-compliance
Lightning Source LLC
Chambersburg PA
CBHW030325100526
44592CB00010B/573